Stay on Course
The Life and Legacy of Ennio Riga, "Chef to the Stars"

Stay on Course
The Life and Legacy of Ennio Riga, "Chef to the Stars"

May you always Stay on Course

Julie Riga

ISBN: 0999164317
ISBN 13: 9780999164310

This book is dedicated to
my grandchildren,
the next generation of
RIGA's

And if the world falls down on your shoulders,
brush it off, and keep going your way.
Stay on Course – Ennio Riga

Contents

A Note from the Editor, Amy Vaughn

First and foremost, I want to thank for allowing me to be a part of the great Ennio Riga journey, as well as her own. I want to thank Ennio Riga himself for gifting me with his book, as well as the countless others who have helped put his dream together, including Colleen, Rose, Ennio's extended family, and his old coworkers, who all helped contribute and fine-tune Ennio's story during my editing process. I also want to thank my mother for introducing me to Julie when she heard Julie was in search of an editor. I will forever be grateful for this opportunity and experience.

To say this project was life-changing does not do it justice. As I traveled on Ennio's course, I found myself analyzing how far I had come myself, where I was heading, and how much faith had helped me stay on my own course. As I read and edited Ennio's life story, it felt as though Ennio was speaking directly to me, bringing me back to life during a time where I found myself a little lost.

Putting Ennio's dream together was not a simple task. Julie, Colleen, and I pored over Ennio's original manuscript, put together by Ennio and his nurse, Maria, both of whom did not speak English as their first language. After constructing it as best we could and breaking it into chapters, I stepped in to smooth out the bumps and allow Ennio's words to shine through to his audience. We pored over countless photographs, recipes, and articles written about Ennio's success, and we watched videos Julie had recorded of her father. We conducted conference calls and asked dozens of people to submit their fond memories of Ennio for our *Reflections* sections. We contacted chefs that Ennio had mentored to help us break down his banquet-style recipes and re-create them as "family size" for those who wish to cook them at home. Julie delved into her father's legacy and leadership to write parts of the book that we have woven into Ennio's story. The process involved various projects going on at once, and while it was overwhelming at times, we had each other's encouragement and Ennio's own passion to help us push onward and *stay on course*. We always beamed with excitement as we pieced everything together on those late evenings after work, chomping away on yummy snacks that Julie, the chef's daughter, always supplied.

Staying on course is a part of me now. Ennio's words filled my mind and found their way into my bloodstream, lighting me up with hope, faith, and inspiration from this man's amazing journey and spirit. In your early twenties, it's hard to figure out what your dreams may be. It's hard to figure out which direction is the "right" direction. Ennio taught me this: to love myself, love my family fully, thank God, trust my instincts, and work hard. Live life with passion, laughter, and of course—great food.

I believe that Mr. Riga's story is everlasting. For Ennio's generation, some aspects of his story may be relatable. For Julie's generation, these are their parents. And for my generation and beyond, this is the story of our grandparents or great-grandparents in the future. As I enter my mid-twenties, I am seeing this generation start to pass, and am realizing the stories that I would listen to on my own grandfather's knee will soon not be told by him. Saying goodbye to family members as they age has been a hard lesson as I grow older. I find myself wishing that they, too, had left books behind, because every life is so incredibly meaningful, and everyone has their own story and legacy to pass on. I believe that Ennio's book is a gift not only to his family but to the world—because the fundamental lessons of staying true to yourself, having faith in God, and staying on course are truly timeless pieces of advice—indeed they are the essence of life.

Introduction: Hellos and Goodbyes

The name *Riga* means "line" in English (it can also mean row, ruler, stripe, rule, parting, streak, rank). Although the Italian translation of *Stay on Course* could be *Rimani sul percorso*, it could also be *Rimani sul Riga*, or "Stay on the Line" (i.e., the straight and narrow).

Hellos

My daughter, Julie, good night, and Grandpa, and don't forget the Five-Fruit Tree.[1] And if the world falls down on your shoulders, brush it off, and keep going your way. Stay on course. Have faith in Jesus, and the Holy Spirit and God, and They will be with you and never, ever let you down from now till eternity.

—*Ennio Riga*

---

1 Inside jokes. See https://www.youtube.com/watch?v=CwtKwzXuWQI

WELCOME. PLEASE MAKE yourself comfortable. Enjoy a cup of coffee as you read this, along with some beautiful background music… maybe some Frank Sinatra.[2]

You are about to experience the life and legacy of my father, Ennio Riga, the most colorful and encouraging person I have ever met. He was and always will be my dad…my coach, mentor, teacher, best friend, and provider. His legacy will forever live on through his children and grandchildren. As I carry both my father's name and face, it is quite fitting for me to shepherd his book, his final dream, to completion.

What's the one thing I miss most about my dad? He was my cheerleader. He believed in me like no one else. When he retired, he told me that he now lived his life through me, and he made it his business to know all about what was going on in my life. We used to dream together of winning the lottery and then discuss all the wonderful ways we would spend the money. It never got old.

My father was always extremely interested and invested in my career. We had a detailed plan for my future and how I was going to achieve bigger and better things. He used to say to me, "Julie, stay on course, stay on course, you are right on track. You are charting well." This book

___

2 https://www.youtube.com/watch?v=H3MqmV47Lq8

is about how my father stayed on *his* course and accomplished amazing feats as a foreigner in a new land, with just a sixth-grade education from Italy.

When my father realized how sick he was, he was determined to capture his life story and not leave this earth until the job was completed. He spent hours talking to his nurse, Maria, who typed his words. If you knew my father, you know he loved to tell stories and did it well. He experienced some incredible adventures. When he passed away on February 12, 2016, I felt compelled to make his story available for everyone to read.

I opened a GoFundMe page to help pay for some of the expenses involved in creating this book for my dad, and received many generous donations. It was amazing to see the outpouring of love from those who knew him. Finishing the work my dad started was a great source of healing to me, because Dad was alive through every word I read. The memories comforted me, and I am so thankful that writing this book helped me cope with such a hard loss.

It may sound silly, but my dad became my best friend when I became an adult. Having a chef as a father is a different type of upbringing. He was working most of my childhood, and I only really saw him on holidays and Sundays.

After college, when Dad opened Riga's restaurant, I started to really know him, even work for him. As a result, we became close—so close that I told him everything that was going on with my life. As I got older and he grew sick, I talked with him even more. It became an everyday ritual.

Talking to my dad was always the highlight of my day. We talked about work, food, and of course, people. I loved that I could talk to the chef any time I needed to cook something. In fact, I used to call my mom and immediately just say, "Can you put Dad on the phone?" Everything he cooked was amazing. Somehow my dad knew how to fix everything with his kind words and warm food.

Although my dad was in Florida and I was in New Jersey, the distance did not stop me from feeling like I was still the most important person in his life. When I did go to Florida, about three times a year, it was an eating extravaganza, and the meal planning went on months before I arrived. My parents would literally call me while I was at work to ask me what I wanted to eat.

We even had a tradition the day I arrived: seafood salad for lunch and ribs for dinner. This was always my favorite day, because I knew my dad would be there with open arms waiting for me, making me feel like I was truly home.

Growing up, people were often so surprised that I did not speak fluent Italian, to which (with great flourish) I would respond: *Mio padre è dell'Italia, ma non mi ha mai insegnato italiano!* This translates to: "My father is from Italy, but he never taught me [how to speak] Italian." I used this dramatic line whenever I wanted something from him. I figured he should feel guilty for not teaching me Italian. This became something we spent hours joking about, and I told this to most of the Italians I met in Italy, since this was the only thing I knew how to say (with dramatic flair, that is). To this day, I wish I knew more Italian.

For the past year or so, I have spent many hours with a team of people to put this book together. I want to give special thanks to Amy Vaughn, who spent countless hours editing and writing to help bring this to life. I also want to thank Colleen Jones for assisting in coordination efforts and design. Special thanks to my trusted chief editorial advisor, Andy O'Hearn, who helped make this book's big-picture messages resonate while also delving deep into the details to make sure they were consistent, complete, and accurate. His innate storytelling sense and grammatical acumen elevated this book to the next level of excellence.

I want to thank every single person who donated funds to help me put this book together. It really helped me start the ball rolling and get the right team involved. I want to thank Maria, my dad's nurse, for sitting with him, listening, and capturing the stories he told. I want to thank my dear husband, Jamie, and my amazing daughter, for giving me space to finish the work that my dad started. Thank you, Rose and Debbie, for working with me to go through stories that helped bring my memories to life. Many thanks to everyone else who contributed in making this book a huge success.

Most of all, I want to thank Dad for giving all of us this gift that will allow us to remember him for years to come.

With all of that being said, it's almost time for you to experience the flavors of my father's life: success, pain, triumphs, and love. But most of all, wherever Ennio was, there was fun. He was silly, kind, welcoming, and (let's face it) an Italian! I say that with the greatest admiration and respect. Dad oozed with passion and fire, which forged an incomparable childhood, career, and family life.

Goodbyes

My dad passed on February 12, 2016. He was in Lake Worth, Florida, and I was in Florham Park, New Jersey, 1,222 miles away. I had planned to leave to see him on Sunday, February 14, but I canceled my trip when he passed. Dad had been diagnosed with stage IV lung cancer almost three years prior to his death. He fought the good fight and tried everything to beat it. He stood in faith and went for chemo and radiation. It was heartbreaking and yet encouraging for me to watch. I never saw someone so hungry to beat cancer until it beat him. We prayed and prayed and believed and stood in our faith and held on. His faith grew and grew. He never stopped believing and was excited to see God and everyone he lost. His mom, dad, and brother were waiting for him, along with Grandpa Sam.

I said goodbye to my dad in person on January 4, 2016. He always woke up before we left in the morning for our flights.

I videotaped him, and what follows below were his words. I can tell you that I have said goodbye to my dad so many times like this, and a few times he acted like it was the last time he would see me. It was so hard to leave him that it stayed with me for days. But this time, I told him he could not do that to me again, so we did not say goodbye like it was the last time... but he did say the words below on video. I gave him a hug and kiss and told him that I loved him and I would see him soon. I told him he was not allowed to cry. I knew in my heart that my dad was not doing well now, but I tried to be hopeful, as I always was.

"Hi everyone! I see you soon. I see you at Julie's wedding. Hello, goodbye! I hope my granddaughter does very well in school, and if you see my granddaughter, tell her I love her and ten times more. And good luck to you, because I love you, and be happy with me or without me. Bye, bye, bye, bye, say hello to everyone. I am a registered Republican, I am an American. Say hello to everyone for the first time and who knows, maybe the last time."

Shortly after recording this message, Dad started to decline fast. Hospice was finally called in to help him transition. None of us realized how quickly he would leave us.

I took a long time to decide when to leave to say goodbye to him. In my heart, I knew that I could not. I wanted to remember him strong, well, and vibrant—the man I had leaned on for strength.

In fact, the last conversation I had with my dad was serious. It was about a week before he died and was probably the last real conversation he had with anyone. I wish I had known that it would be the last time I would really speak to him on the phone. It was serious and fun, just like my dad. We even sang together some of the songs he would sing to me as a child and that we always sang just to have fun. My dad was not around much growing up at night, but he would sing us songs and put us to bed.

My sweetheart, my daughter, remember, there is no one sillier than me. Oh, no, wait, you are really the funny one. You have a lot of children to take care of now. You must look after my six grandchildren and my nephews, your sister, and Barbara. Make sure you stay in touch with your Italian family; all of them. Keep an eye on them to make sure everyone is well. Tell them I love them.

The week before my dad died, my sister Devorah (Debbie) did not leave his side. She Face-timed me with him so I could see them both, and we spent hours together on the phone. I felt as though I was there. I spoke and sang to him while she talked with him and comforted him. Debbie was there when he passed over. She said it was such a beautiful moment and that she felt his spirit leave his body. Debbie sensed that they were not alone, that he went very quickly into the gates of heaven to be reunited with his family and God, where he would have no more pain.

While Debbie was in Florida experiencing this, I was at Legal Seafood having an early Valentine's Day dinner with my husband, Jamie, because I had planned to leave for Florida that following Sunday. I ordered my dad's favorite meal: the fried seafood platter. Oh, he loved that. I stayed connected by phone with my sister and wanted to stay on the phone while I was eating, but my sister said his breathing was labored. It was hard to grasp what was about to happen. I was about to lose my dad, my coach, and my best friend. This was a moment I will never forget. My heart was broken.

After this, I canceled my flight. My dad was being cremated, and we planned on having a memorial service a few months later. Dad had always told me, "Julie, stay on course, stay on course, stay on course."

I took a few days to cry. One day, I had a meltdown at Trader Joe's. The cashier asked me how I was, and with tears I said, "I just lost my dad." You know that when you tell someone you just lost your parent, you get his or her story about losing his or her parent. I guess it is a bond that brings us all together.

Losing my dad was a defining moment in my life. I decided that I was going to be an authentic griever. I was going to cry spontaneously when I wanted to, and I was going to be aware that, wherever I go, I would carry my dad's legacy: one of strength, courage, hope, family, and fun.

My dad left me at a time when things were going well. I was about to be married to a wonderful man; I had just gotten hired for an amazing job where I would train executives on leadership. My daughter was getting all A's in school. The only struggle I had to deal with was his loss. I was getting married that April, and he was supposed to be there. Not having him there was hard.

The week after he died, I decided to make his final request come true. My dad dreamed of writing his life story. He wanted his own book to tell the tales of his crazy, amazing journey to this country. He wanted everyone to know about all of the incredible people he met along the way. He met some great ones and worked with some even better ones. He spoke so highly of so many people: his favorite boss, David Simon, and others from Prime Hospitality, like Peter Marino, Don Corbosiero, Brenda Sara, Rich Bennett, Bill Kuruc (recipe editing and coordination), Bob Garvey, Wayne Ricco (executive chefs), Tim Lauch, Sam Calello, Gary Gabriele, Rosalie Chierkove, and all of his staff at Riga, whom he truly adored. You all exemplified the intersection of excellence, passion, and creativity. May you be blessed tenfold for your kind contributions.

And who could forget the New Jersey wedding DJ entertainer, Michael Scalisi, with whom my dad loved to sing? I remember many times we watched Ennio flambé—so much fun.

It was not hard to decide that my next "big rock" (for those of you who know about the 7 Habits of Highly Effective People, one of my favorite leadership books) was to complete his story in book form for everyone to read. He worked with his nurse tirelessly to capture this story, and had about one hundred pages (in a very large type size) of great stories left for me to edit and for you to enjoy.

With a new marriage, new job, and an active child, most of my days were filled. How could I possibly pull this together in a relatively short time? I needed to hire help, and the only thing standing in my way was money. That was where the GoFundMe page came in. We received some donations from people who knew and loved my dad. These kind donations helped me to hire a book coordinator and editor, while my husband Jamie stepped in to provide much-needed help organizing and scanning materials. My daughter and husband truly supported me on this journey, and I thank them for that. My editor and I sat next to each other and read Ennio's thoughts out loud, worked on rewrites, and spent lots of time on the phone with my mother, Rose.

I spent hours learning more about my dad to help bring these stories to you as accurately as possible. I hope his words inspire you in some way. His message to you is Stay On Course: follow the dreams you have for your life. He showed this over and over again in his determination to make something great of himself—something so great that his amazing legacy carries on through his family, friends, and colleagues.

Over this past year, some amazingly sacred moments let me know that my dad was with me. On Father's Day, I decided to stay home and miss dinner with my husband's family because I was thinking of Dad so much. Although Dad was gone, I was going to spend the day with him. I cooked sauce, listened to Italian music, and can remember saying to myself, "If 'Volare' comes on next, I know my dad is with me. Well, "Volare" came on next, and I just bawled. Then, with my eyes closed, I started to dance as though he was dancing with me. My dad never got to dance with me at my wedding, but I believe we did have our final dance on Father's Day. I know this sounds silly, but it was incredibly comforting.

One day, on my way to the office, I came across a random Roma tomato on the ground. I stood there, shocked. I thought, *Why is there a Roma tomato near the door at work?* I went upstairs and asked Kristen, my great friend and colleague, to come downstairs with me to see if it was really there. I thought I might have been seeing things. But sure enough, it was there, and I took it as a sign from Dad. I feel him with me most when I am at work, maybe because I know that he was so proud of my accomplishments. The year he died, I created a leadership program for executives, and he would have loved to have heard all about the program and how this teaching influenced others for good.

A few months later, I walked outside the front door of my house. I do not use my front door much, because my family usually enters and exits from the garage. I turned the corner and found a random tomato plant growing right in front of my house…hundreds of cherry tomatoes were growing on a vine that no one had planted. I was shocked and so surprised. I called my neighbors and asked them if they knew anything about this. I wondered if they had planted it—but they hadn't, and they were just as surprised that this random plant was growing rapidly right by our homes. I told them how Dad's logo at Riga's was the tomato. Was my dad trying to remind me of what he had always told me? "Julie, though I will not be with you, I will always be with you. I will watch over you from the other side." Throughout the year I even saw some interesting things in the sky that reminded me once again that my Dad is with me.

I was checking Dad's Facebook page recently, which I do not do often, and came across a message to Dad from exactly a year before:

Good afternoon, Chef Riga, you may not remember me at all. Many years ago, you came to oversee the Marriott Hotel in downtown Baltimore for a few weeks. I will never forget you, and your friendly, kind disposition. You did NOT show any prejudice to anyone. You treated the kitchen staff with respect, and you have a wonderful sense of humor. You showed me, and the Garde/manager staff, how to make vegetable crudités a different way, because we were using too many vegetables. I remember your tomato and goat cheese platter with olive oil and garlic and fresh basil. Very delicious. God bless you, Chef Ennio Riga.

What a gift to see this! This person probably has no idea that her kind words made the book. It was just another testament to Dad's character and expertise. She said she would never forget him, and I am sure most of you who knew him will never forget him either.

Viva the chef—my dad, my coach, my friend, and my provider. All of the good I am, and all of the good I do, is because I knew you. I have been changed for good because of you. Not a day goes by that I do not think about you or how I carry your legacy with me. How I want to share my successes and my struggles with you, but somehow, I know you are, and always will be, with me.

I love you, Dad.

Ending Prayer

Rest in peace, my daddy, Rest in peace.
Your legacy lives, you are in our hearts
Always and our thoughts.

I thank you for the wealth of your wisdom.
I thank you for being my leader, my friend, my coach, my
teacher.
I thank you for your strong unwavering faith and showing
me the power,
the strength, and the love of God.
I thank you for loving me and believing in me.
I thank you for giving me a true gift of understanding:
that I am worthy of good things, and love and blessings
from God.
I will miss you every day, and you will go with me
through every success and every failure…

**And if the world falls down on my shoulders, I will keep
going.**
I will stay on course. I will live as a Riga.
Because the Riga's are a strong. We never die. We live on.
We transcend earth to heaven, to be with God.

xxx

The sting of death has been overcome by the power of God, and I will see you again.

I look forward to the day I can see you again. I love you!

Though you are not here, your Legacy lives on:

Colorful, vibrant, powerful, smart, full of influence.

As you asked, I will watch over all of your nieces and nephews and grandchildren.

I will help to guide them as you did, and I am honored to continue your legacy.

Rest in peace, dear Daddy.

Remember me as you dance on streets of gold and cook for everyone.

We celebrate your life in honor. In Jesus's name, Amen.

CHAPTER 1

❧

Italy: 1938 – 1951

JOIN ME AT my table while I tell you the story of my life—an extraordinary journey. *Sedetevi (Sit)*. Have some food. Stay awhile.

This book has been my dream for a long, long time. Please allow me to share the joys, the pains, and the victories of this amazing path I've traveled.

I am Ennio Giuseppe Riga, son of Pasqua De Tina and Angelo Riga. I was born on July 18, 1938, in a village in northeast Italy named Zompicchia (belonging to the municipality of Codroipo, in the province of Udine, region Friuli-Venezia Giulia).

I was raised in a small and modest 150-year-old country home, which my father purchased prior to my birth for only three thousand *lire* (roughly $1.73 or 1.55 euros in today's currency).

I was born on a hot, muggy day. Humid summers were typical of this area, called *Pianura Padana*—perhaps you have heard of Grana Padano cheese, which comes from the same area. As the sun shone down brightly, the umbilical cord wrapped itself around my neck, and the midwife who was assisting my mother could not deliver me. They had to rush me to the nearest hospital, which was located a few miles from our village, in Codroipo. My mother nearly died from excessive bleeding. I was turning blue and covered with bruises. But *grazie a dio (Thank God)*, we both survived.

The height of World War II was a very difficult time for all of us, but we did the best we could to survive and live well. With little money or food to go around, times were hard—which made life full of challenges…or opportunities, which was how I chose to look at it. I have tried to turn difficult times into opportunities all my life.

To assist my family, I worked at an early age. I cannot remember a time in my life when I did not work. Since I was small, I attended to our country house. We had seven *polli* (chickens), two *mucche* (cows), and an *asino* (donkey). I would tend to all of them and help my mother in the fields while my father worked.

My mother, Pasqua, was the hero of my life. The women in World War II were so brave—they protected and maintained the households while the men were away. They remained fiercely strong as the war began to take over our very villages, or *villaggi*. My father, Angelo, was also a hard-working man and someone I looked up to greatly. When he was only eighteen years old, he left Italy and went to Canada to make a living. My father made a fortune, but in 1929, he lost all of his savings when the Great Depression hit. He returned to Italy and bought our little country house with the money he had left. In 1934, my parents married.

At home, my mother was the boss. She ran the whole establishment like a tight ship. Every time my father came home late, my mother would hit him. He had to be home by five-thirty every evening to *mungere le mucche*, or milk the cows. If my father was late, then milking the cows fell to my mother. But even though she was stern, my mother loved us all so much.

I had the pleasure of learning at a young age that my mother always meant business, *faceva sul serio*. She most certainly earned the "boss" title. One warm summer day when I was young, I stole an *uovo* (egg) from our *pollaio* (henhouse). I was hungry, and dinner was a few hours away. As I crept out of the henhouse, my mother caught me. Her face reddened with rage. She flew back into the house and called the *carabinieri*, the police. She told them to take me to *prigione* (jail)

The police arrived and greeted my mother while I stood frozen with fear. They put handcuffs on me as my mother watched with her arms folded, her anger radiating off of her like heat. The police took me to the *prigione* in our *villaggio*. I was scared to death. My mother had sent me to *prigione*! For stealing an *uovo*!

An hour later, my mother came and picked me up. As we walked out of the *prigione*, she turned to me and looked at me sharply. *"Hai visto cosa succeed a chi ruba?"* ("See what happens to those who steal?")

୬

By 1943, the *Nazisti* started to increase the brutality in our area. One day, a family appeared at our doorstep and asked us to hide them from the *Nazisti*. The Germans had already captured the father, so we hid the mother, teenage son, and young daughters. The son eventually left and went to join the Partisans to help fight against the *Nazisti*. He was later killed in combat. Only the mother and daughters remained in our care. We had a cellar where they would hide during the day. It was complete with a tunnel passage for access to fresh air and food. At night, they would come into the house to sleep. This went on for almost two years. No one ever found them.

On most days during the war, my parents would go to work in the fields and leave me behind at home. They were afraid the Germans would shoot me. It became unsafe to leave home or stray too far. But together, we tried to hold on as the chaos of the war infiltrated our home and garden.

When the *Nazisti* took control of our *villaggio*, danger permeated the air daily. But that did not quiet the desire for me to help the less fortunate who were suffering before my eyes.

One morning, my mother put aside five *uova* for a frittata dinner. When she went to gather the *uova* in the evening, however, she only found three…because I had thrown two *uova* over the fence to the starving children who lived across from our garden. My heart would break for them. Something bigger than myself, something that filled me with courage and purpose, told me to help them. I could not watch them starve in front of me.

I had to confess to my mother that I threw the *uova* to the children. My mother smacked me and sent me to bed without dinner. My mother thought that she was teaching me another lesson, but the next day I did it again. I believed I was doing the right thing.

You see, I was hungry…but they were starving.

The second floor of our home held a large bedroom window. My mother would always tell me not to get too close to it. *Soldati (Soldiers)* were within our view, and she wanted us to be scarcely seen. But I was a child and did not listen. Early one morning, I disobeyed and looked through the window. A German *soldato* saw me and shot at my head. The bullet grazed my skull as it soared through the wide window. The force knocked me to the ground, and blood erupted from the wound. The bullet went straight into the second-floor wall and lodged itself there, where it remains to this day. My mother was terrified, because she thought I would die from the wound. After it was confirmed that I would survive, however, she beat me for disobeying her. I was saved by a miracle that day. I have carried the scar of the bullet on my head my entire life.

A few days after I was injured, the *Nazisti* were at our door. They took my father because he had a Canadian passport and sent him to make bombs in a factory called Mangiarotti in Codroipo. I was terrified that they had taken my father prisoner, but my mother once more stood strong and held us all together in his absence.

By 1944, the *Nazisti* started to get desperate because the Americans were winning the war. My father was still being held prisoner. One day, a bomb exploded by accident at Mangiarotti and the factory was destroyed. My father was stuck

> Years before, during World War II, when his father refused to salute the Nazis and their Fascist allies, he was abducted and sent to German concentration camps. In defiance, Riga's family sheltered Jews and others fleeing the growing Nazi tyranny. Riga says he was 5 years old when he saw his father stumbling toward the house, with his teeth torn out, his ribs broken and weighing less than 100 pounds. He had escaped a forced-labor camp after the Americans had bombed it and he had walked for 40 days to come back home. World War II ended soon after that.
>
> "But I saw around me so much starvation, so much hunger that I decided if there was to be no show biz, I would go into the food business. You may not make money, but you always eat."

under the debris, but he and two others survived. After the bombing, they were able to escape. They only traveled the distance back to our *villagio* at night to avoid capture. We had to hide them alongside the family that we were already protecting from the *Nazisti*.

Six people were hiding in the cellar and tunnel. Adding my mother, my sister, and me, nine people were cramped and avoiding capture in our tiny home.

Before each visit, the SS Gestapo would routinely case the house for food and escapees, and my mother would begin to hit me. My house was on the suspects list. Tension ran high at these anticipated inspections. My mother would do anything to protect all of us. Even hit her son.

"I'm sorry, son, I'm sorry," she would say.

"Why are you beating me?" I wailed.

"It's so when you see the *Nazisti,* you start to cry," she said.

As soon as the *Nazisti* arrived, I was already crying and hysterical.

She would stand tall and say, *"Visto cosa suddede a mio figlio? Piange ogni volta (che vi vede)! Uscite subito di qui!"* ("See what happens to my son? He cries each time he sees you! Get out now!")

My mother said she was doing this to save our lives. After the *Nazisti* left, she would hug me and ask me to forgive her. I always did.

⅌

I went to school in 1944. It was a tough year, because of the German invasion. Our school was right by the church, on *Via Delle Scuole*, School Road. It was a beautiful building with a colonnaded patio. Our teachers were mostly young women, some as young as fourteen. Because they were in constant fear over the occupation, we learned very little. If you went to school, you had to wear the *Nazista grembiulino*, Nazi school uniform, in all black. They had infiltrated every aspect of our lives during their occupation and control of the village.

We all prayed for the Americans to come. We waited and waited. We heard whispers that their arrival was nearing and that we would be protected from the *Nazisti*.

When the Americans finally came, the *Nazisti* had to escape by foot. They would put their hands up and yell, *"Non sparate!"* ("Don't shoot!")

On one of the days when they were fleeing, the Germans were in front of our house, hiding from the Americans by the door. When I opened the front door, a *Nazista* fell over me. He was already dead. My mother dragged him out on the street and rushed to close the door.

༒

After the war ended, things were still very difficult: no money, no well-paying jobs, no food, and no textiles. This extreme hardship drove several Italians to migrate abroad. Many people from Zompicchia and Codroipo moved to France, Germany, Switzerland, the United States, and many other countries in search of employment and opportunities. My father tried his best but was not very productive under all of the stress. One afternoon during this time, I told my father that I had to study before class.

"*Non suonerai piu il violino,*" he said. You will not play the violin anymore.

"*Perchè?*" I asked. ("Why?")

"Because you don't have a violin anymore," he said. My father broke it over my head. I wailed.

"*Ora Puoi andare a lavorare nei campi.*" ("Now you can go work in the fields.") And so I did.

༒

In 1946, my mother had another boy, my beloved baby brother, Galdino. He was such a joy to me. In his young years, he was weak, probably due to the little food or care that was available due to the war. By the time he was one, Galdino had polio. We struggled a lot that year. We loved that boy. He was *un cosi bel bambino* (such a beautiful child) In our *villagio*, many children were dying from polio. Thankfully, by the grace of God, Galdino grew up to be a healthy and good man.

I finished elementary school when I was ten, in July 1948. Since times were so hard, my father demanded that I work to help support the family, especially with the addition of my little brother. My father sent me to work for Il Signor Gigi, a wine distributor. Every day I would begin delivering wine for Il Signor Gigi at six a.m. In Italy, many people would *fare un pisolino*, take a nap, in the afternoon. Since I had so many responsibilities between Il Signor Gigi and home, I would chop wood for the winter during the hours people rested. Afterward, from three to eight p.m., I would go back to delivering wine. Suddenly, I was putting in fourteen-hour days.

When I arrived home at night, I was so tired I could not eat. I was losing weight remarkably fast, because I did not have the energy to eat dinner and was overworked. On most days, I would come home, eat a piece of polenta, and fall right to sleep.

It was common at that time for children to have jobs. Boys as young as I was, between eight and ten, would work in fields, in the few factories or shops nearby, and as errand boys. Girls often worked as seamstresses, house cleaners, or at the local spinning mill. Soon after the war, most parents ignored the importance of school. Children would generally attend kindergarten and the first three years of elementary school, and then they would be expected to begin working.

It was my responsibility to help my family. Delivering wine, however, was not easy. They would put 140 pounds of wine in containers on my shoulders to carry. This caused me so much anxiety. I was sure that if I fell, I'd lose my job. One day, the *damigiana* fell on me. I couldn't breathe and broke some ribs. Luckily, the *damigiana* did not break. (*damigiana*: a large container that holds wine; a bulbous, narrow-necked bottle holding from three to ten gallons of liquid, typically enclosed in a wicker cover)

During this time, I was making about one dollar a week (the equivalent of eleven dollars in 2017) and would bring it home for my father. This job was too hard for me. I worked six days a week for fourteen hours a day. The worst part was the *inverno*, the winter. I was also responsible for getting *le interiora di agnello e di maiale*, the lamb and pork guts, to make the *salami e salsicce*, salami and sausages, with my family. They smelled rotten. It wasn't something I wanted to be doing after working all day long.

After witnessing me working like a madman, a friend of our family called my father. He told him that they were killing me with too much work and to get me out of working for Il Signor Gigi. My father did not want me to stop working, but his friend said, "Don't be a fool. A week from now, your son may be dead. Get him out of there." My father finally let me stop working for Il Signor Gigi, but he was angry at the loss of income.

At age eleven, I went to work at a local restaurant called Bar Scagnetti. I was responsible for cleaning the floor, stocking the shelves, and working in the wine room. My boss would never go into the wine room, because he was afraid of dying in there. The wine room was at the very back of the building and was very dangerous. We had to be very careful while we were there, because all kinds of poisons were present in the chemical fumes. After the war, little soap was available, so we used bleach, muriatic (hydrochloric) acid, and more to clean. Prolonged exposure to these fumes in the wine room was extremely dangerous— especially because we rinsed the *damigiana* with those same chemicals.

One day, Benito, one of the older boys who worked with me, went into the wine room and did not come out. I went to look for him and found him sprawled on the floor. His uniform had been destroyed from the chemicals. He had broken a *damigiana* that contained fifty liters of bleach and passed out from the gas. I dragged him out of the wine room and saved his life.

After working there for a while, I proved myself valuable to my boss, and he gave me a permanent job. I was proud of my hard work and my family needed the security.

Un sera d'inverno (a winter night), I was working and I thought I heard the sound of choking from the toilet, adjacent to the wine room. I went to check but couldn't open the door or see anybody through the glass window on the top of the door. I went to the service lady, Paula, and asked her who was in the toilet. She said it was Mirta, my boss's sixteen-year-old daughter. The door was locked from the inside. I managed to eventually break the door handle and shove the door open. Mirta lay passed out on the floor, her head right by the entryway of the bathroom. I picked her up and carried her in my arms to get her to safety while her parents called for a doctor. At this particular time, I was about thirteen. I was strong from carrying such heavy items at a young age, and Mirta's weight did not bother me.

When the doctor arrived, he told me: *"Giovanotto, ancora un minuto e sarebbe morta per le esalazioni del gas."* ("Young man, one more minute and she would be dead from the gas leak.")

That year, I saved two lives. After I saved his daughter's life, my boss fired the other employees and gave me a raise.

I learned the restaurant business with Il Signor Scagnetti. He paid me ten dollars a month (about ninety-four dollars today). I worked the bar and delivered food after work for extra tips, which were my little secret. I never told my father, because he would have taken them from me. As time went on, other people noticed my hard work and began offering me jobs.

When I was fourteen, I went to work at the COOP, a big grocery store chain; I was finally legally allowed to work. The money was good enough to support my family and buy groceries. I continued to pocket the tips I made delivering food for myself.

At sixteen, I started a soccer team with my friend Dorino. I managed to get the best players in the village. I would use the tip money for shirts and team supplies. We went to the finals, but the other team cheated and won. Some of the players from my soccer team went on to play professional soccer. Besides work and my family, I really enjoyed playing soccer.

In 1955, I was seventeen. Three more COOPs opened, and I was in charge of coordinating the *consegne del cibo*, the food delivery. Every Friday in Italy, customers would come and make a reservation for *baccalà*, the traditional Italian dried and salted *merluzzo*, codfish. One morning, around nine, a woman came to the store with her husband. Her husband was a North American F100 Super Sabre pilot at the local airport, Rivolto, a military base. I would see the planes flying overhead almost every day. We made small talk before they ordered two pounds of *baccalà* to be delivered to their home later that day.

That afternoon, I biked over to deliver their *baccalà*. The wife opened the door and thanked me as I handed her their order. I asked the wife where her husband was. She pointed above my shoulder toward the sky. Planes soared across the brilliant blue above us.

"My husband is flying today. I have to cook because he's coming home for lunch." She smiled at me. The wife was pretty, young, and seven months pregnant, with a swollen stomach. I wished her well and turned to go back to the COOP to complete my daily deliveries.

On my way back, I looked up and watched four planes soar right above me. Suddenly, to my horror, the last plane's right wing caught fire. The plane plummeted before my eyes, from where I was standing toward the homes across the *Torrente Corno*, a stream (Valley of the Horn torrent).

The plane crashed and erupted in flames as it hit one of the homes, landing in the center of Zompicchia. We later learned that the lady who owned the house had not been home, and that the plane's pilot had deviated his route to avoid the primary school.

Immediately, I started pedaling my bike to cross the *Torrente Corno* and reach the accident. I saw a priest trying to get there as well. He was unable to make it very far. When he saw me pedaling nearby, he called to me for help.

I rushed into the water toward the priest and fumbled as I wrapped my arms around him. His clothing was heavy, weighing him down and slowing his trek across the creek. The only thing I could attempt to do was lift him up. The priest was so heavy, he felt like a thousand pounds.

I said to him, "I don't think I can make it."

Then he said, "*Si, ce la farai, abbi fede!*" ("Yes. You will make it. Have faith.")

I don't know how, but we miraculously made it to the other side, despite his weighty clothing and the flowing water. My faith was lifted. Unfortunately, by the time the *prete* and I emerged from the water, the house was enflamed and falling to the ground. The pilot did not make it.

When the rescue team finally pulled him from the fallen wreckage, I was saddened to recognize him as the man who had been in my store that morning buying *baccalà* with his wife. The rescue team asked if anyone knew where his wife was.

"I just came from there," I said.

"Will you come with me to tell his wife about the accident?" the *poliziotto*, the policeman, asked me. I could not say no. Together, we left the scene to deliver the horrible news to the pretty young woman I had seen just an hour before. Up until this point, this was probably the hardest thing I had to do in my life. I was heartbroken for her: they were expecting their first child, and this tragedy happened right before my eyes. Together, the *poliziotto* and I delivered the news, and she wept in front of us. My heart felt for her deeply.

Julie's Reflections

I grew up with two foreigners as parents. I am a first-generation American. My Catholic dad, as you now know, was from northern Italy. On my Jewish mother's side, I have a Russian Jewish grandmother, and she met my Polish Jewish grandfather in the woods as they journeyed together to escape the Nazis. My mother, Rose, was born somewhere in Siberia (allegedly) and then when she was five, she came to America with her parents and twin siblings.

15

What a crazy beginning we all had! Dad and Mom's families were at the mercy of a terrible war, and it was something that stayed with them for a long time. I cannot even imagine what my grandparents and Mom had to endure. The one thing I do know is that they were survivors, and so was Dad. My dad came to America with no family and made a beautiful life for himself. A portion of Mom's extended family came to America, and we spent most holidays with them. We had cousins, second cousins, and even some Gubiners (a group of people from Gubin, Poland that united together as family when everyone lost theirs during the war) who stayed with us through this journey and who became our extended family.

I am Ennio Giuseppe Riga, son of Pasqua De Tina and Angelo Riga.

I was born on July 18, 1938, in a village in northeast Italy named Zompicchia (belonging to the municipality of Codroipo, in the province of Udine, region Friuli–Venezia Giulia).

Leadership Lesson 1:
How to Leave a Lasting Legacy 1A

The literal definition of a legacy is something (often property or money) received from someone who has passed on…an inheritance.

I did not get money when Dad died, but I did get an inheritance that cannot be measured. When talking about this book, my boss asked me such a profound question (thank you, Marketta). She asked me, "Julie, what did your father leave you?" It made me stop and think…and was exactly the question I needed to be asked to prompt me to write this. My dad left me a lifetime of lessons and an unassailable confidence…as well as the drive to share what that means, so that others could benefit from it.

The Chef often joked with me, because he claimed to have brainwashed me with his mindset…to believe I could do anything I put my mind to with hard work. That all things were possible. That I was worthy of good things. Somehow, just knowing he was there to listen to me and stand by me gave me the courage to do more and be more.

I am not saying that my dad and I did not disagree or fight at times, but he believed in me. No matter how many times I messed up, or how many times I wanted to give up, he never gave up knowing that I had all that it took to overcome anything in my path. The strength he exemplified for me was what I needed to overcome some very hard times.

I basically "broke" two times in my life. I know we all break at some point, and I believe it makes us stronger. The only difference for me was that my amazing father walked with me through everything. He was there to listen, encourage, and coach. Dad never rescued me from the world's hardness, but he was there to walk with me through it. This made it easy for me to believe in God, because Dad was such an incredible example of God's love!

No matter what people said, or how I failed, Dad taught me the following:

- You are strong.
- You are creative and brilliant, and have greatness on the inside.
- Never give up.
- Follow your dreams.
- Never look back.
- If the world falls down on your shoulders, brush it off, and keep going on your way. *Stay on course!*
- Dream big—I mean, *really* big.
- You can't change a donkey into a thoroughbred.
- Go to college.
- Take chances.
- Be diplomatic.
- If you love your job, you will never work a day in your life.
- Have fun along the way; laugh, be silly.
- Family comes first.
- *Leave a legacy.*

When I first approached my dad about writing this book, I suggested to him that we do a book together. He hated this idea (ha), because all his life he wanted to write his *own* book. He wanted to share his story, because he believed that people needed to hear from him. He wanted to touch people's hearts and help them to see that anyone *can* overcome hardship.

Dad was such a big dreamer. Not only did he want to do a book, he also wanted to have a TV series and a movie as well! He always told me he had several books inside of him. At the end, he was very sick, but he knew he needed to get his story done fast. We fought about this. Dad was an amazing person, but, when he wanted something, he did not give up. After I agreed that I would help him write his own book, he calmed down. As my dad got older, he calmed down a lot. He was a fiery Italian man with tons of drive and discipline. He really was excited about life and the opportunities it could offer.

Most of all, he taught me to be the best you that you can be, and show up with a great attitude. Make people comfortable and develop a relationship with them. When you are a leader, teach others to soar like an eagle. Nothing is impossible in this life. If you do not believe anything is possible, you will limit yourself. Do not take yourself too seriously. Fun must be a priority also.

֍

Leadership Lesson:
How to Leave a Lasting Legacy 1B

One of my favorite stories my dad told was when, through a terrible sickness, he visited heaven. While he was there, he was embraced by love and God's peace. His loved ones told him, "Your *mission* has not been completed; you must go back." This story stuck with me. We are here for a reason—and each of our reasons or missions are unique. A mission can be a task or job you are assigned, or it could take on a more religious meaning. If you are asking what your life's purpose is, a few questions below will help you start to think about this.

Afterward, my father became more spiritual and realized that he had something to complete: this book. When he got sick, he talked about it all the time and asked for my help. I struggled to figure out how to get his book done…but my dad had a plan. He knew that if he could just write down the stories, he could leave them behind him. He asked his nurse to help, and they worked for months capturing these stories. I also captured some stories on video when I visited him.

I learned that leaving something of yourself behind for those who love you matters. I have learned so much about my father by working on this book; it has been a true gift. Write your stories down; help keep your family's legacy alive.

Here are some thought-provoking questions to get you started:

- Why does my life matter?
- What is my life's mission?
- What am I passionate about?
- What legacy am I leaving behind?
- If someone were writing your life story after you passed on, what would they say about you? What would you *want* them to say about you?
- Did you "stay on course"? If so, how did you accomplish this? Could others replicate (at least in part) some of the lessons you learned? If so, which lessons, and how might they replicate these in their own way?

Chef Table Dinners from Ennio's Notebook
Menu 1

~ Antipasti ~
Calamari Freschi

Tender rings of poached calamari marinated in extra-virgin olive oil and a squeeze of fresh lemon, tossed with roasted red pepper and onion, and seasoned with fresh basil and a hint of garlic.

Served chilled with some crusty French bread.

~ Insalata ~
Panzanella

Baby field greens and tomatoes tossed in balsamic and caper vinaigrette, topped with crumbled goat cheese and cubes of fresh focaccia bread.

~ Entrée ~
Pollo Bell'Anna

Chicken cutlets sautéed with shiitake mushrooms and sun-dried tomatoes, deglazed with sherry wine and chicken stock, and finished with a rich brown sauce and butter.

Serve over your favorite pasta or alongside a rice pilaf.

Menu 1

CALAMARI FRESCHI
(appetizer; serves 4)

Ingredients:

1.5 pounds	Calamari tubes only (sliced into approx. ½" rings)
1 teaspoon	Fresh garlic (chopped)
3 ounces	Extra-virgin olive oil
2 ounces	Roasted red peppers (diced)
2 ounces	Red onion (diced small)
1 tablespoon	Chopped Italian flat-leaf parsley
1 tablespoon	Chopped basil
1 each	Lemon (squeeze juice from 1 lemon)
1 ounce	Red wine vinegar
1 each	Lemon (cut in quarters for garnish)
To taste	Salt and pepper

Preparation:

- Poach calamari in lightly salted water until tender; then chill. Be careful not to overcook, or the calamari will be rubbery. (Poaching liquid can be water only, or you can add white wine and some lemon juice.)

- In a large bowl, combine all other ingredients listed (except for lemon wedges). Toss with calamari and chill.
- Cover and hold in refrigerator until ready to eat. Plate and serve with a lemon wedge and some sliced crusty Italian bread.

PANZANELLA
(insalata; serves 4)

Ingredients:

16 ounces	Mixed baby greens
1 ounce	Red onion (sliced)
10 each	Cherry tomatoes (cut in half)
3 cups	Focaccia bread (cut into crouton-size cubes)
5 to 6 ounces	Goat cheese (crumbled)
¾ cup	Extra-virgin olive oil
¼ cup	Balsamic vinegar
2 teaspoons	Capers
1 tablespoon	Fresh basil (chopped)
To taste	Salt and black pepper

Preparation:

- In a small bowl, place olive oil, balsamic vinegar, capers, chopped basil, and salt and pepper. Whisk together until well-blended.
- In a large mixing bowl, place baby greens, red onion, and cherry tomato halves, and toss with the basil capers vinaigrette you just prepared, to taste.
- Divide salad equally between four plates, top with focaccia cubes and goat cheese, and serve.

This is a traditional central Italy recipe and a popular summer dish. It is made of one-day-old bread soaked in water and then squeezed dry, fresh chopped tomatoes, Italian extra-virgin olive oil, vinegar, salt, pepper, and a leaf of basil on top.

Pollo Bell'Anna
(serves 4)

Ingredients:

8	Chicken cutlets pounded flat and seasoned with salt and pepper (about 4 ounces each)
2 ounces	Extra-virgin olive oil
2 ounces	Sherry wine
4 ounces	Shiitake mushrooms (julienned)
1 ounce	Sun-dried tomatoes (julienned)
6 ounces	Chicken stock
6 ounces	Brown sauce (gravy)
2 ounces	Butter (cut into four pieces)
To taste	Salt and pepper

Preparation:

- Heat a large sauté pan on medium/high heat. Add olive oil and brown chicken breast on both sides.
- Add shiitake mushrooms and cook until soft.
- Add sherry wine to deglaze pan, and then add sun-dried tomatoes, chicken stock, brown sauce, and salt and pepper.
- Bring to a simmer and let cook for a few minutes.

- Just before removing from the stovetop, turn off the heat and stir in butter until incorporated in the sauce.
- Plate two pieces of chicken breast per portion and top with sauce.
- Best served over your favorite pasta or with rice pilaf.

CHAPTER 2

— ❧ —

Switzerland: 1959 – 1962

INSTEAD OF JOINING the Italian army, I continued working to help support my family. Another opportunity for work arose. One day my friend, Benito, came to visit me from Switzerland. He invited me to travel back with him and work with him at the Hotel Helvetia.

I had to make a difficult choice. Moving to Switzerland would mean that I would have to leave behind my family and beautiful girlfriend, Germana, whom I had met in church when I was thirteen. We were so in love, we would just sit and gaze at each other all the time. Germana was the love of my life back then. Even so, I had to consider my future and how I would make money. This was an opportunity I decided I could not miss, so I went to Switzerland and this decision altered my course forever. I left behind everything and everyone I knew. Soon after I left Italy, Germana married a dentist and had three children.

❧

Excited and nervous, I arrived in Switzerland and began working at the Hotel Helvetia. Mr. Croschiane, the owner of the hotel, was an incredible man. I started off at the bottom, working as their dishwasher. But Hotel Helvetia was where I began to really learn. The first thing I was taught to make was ice cream. Soon after that, Mr. Croschiane gave me the chance to work in the kitchen and taught me how to cook vegetables. After mastering the vegetables, I was taught by some of the best chefs how to properly cook fish, which is a specialty in Switzerland. I felt like I was finally moving up in the world.

Working in Switzerland proved to be my destiny. I went from dishwashing to the head of the staff within six months. Mr. Croschiane really valued me and trusted me. So much so that he would ask me to get his special $500 wine (worth more than $4,100 today) and bring it to him. I had a hunger for learning everything. My future stretched in front of me. I was a perfectionist and in love with the process.

A year into my time at the hotel, Mr. Croschiane got married. He was fifty years old and his wife was just nineteen. A little while after they were married, she attempted to have an affair with me. I refused her advances because I loved Mr. Croschiane. He had given me so many opportunities to learn, and I would never disrespect him in such a way. I honored marriage and loyalty. In retaliation, she went to Mr. Croschiane and told him that I tried to have sex with her.

Mr. Croschiane approached me and said, "I cannot fire her because she's my wife. So I have to let you go."

I was fired … and devastated.

HOTEL LA PALMA (LOCARNO, SWITZERLAND, 1959 – 1960)

Despite losing my job, I pressed onward. I found a job in a better place. I went to work in a five-star hotel, La Palma. I was only twenty-one and in charge of the bar. The ambassador of Portugal owned the hotel at the time.

Every August, La Palma hosted a film festival with stars from all over Europe. The tradition had begun in 1946, and each year it was gaining more recognition and prestige.

One evening, a beautiful movie star from Germany saw me working and said, "Young man, my granddaughter is with me and she never goes out. Could you be a gentleman and take her to a movie?"

"Of course, I will be a gentleman," I said, grinning. Who would say no to that?

The hotels closed in the winter, so I went back to Italy for a visit. I made sure to stop and see my friend Joe, who told me some train companies were hiring. He suggested I interview immediately. I arranged for an interview and fortunately was hired.

And suddenly, I was an employee of an international train, the Orient Express.

THE ORIENT EXPRESS (BASEL, SWITZERLAND, 1960–1962)

When I went to work at the Orient Express in 1960, I learned that serving on an international train is quite different from working in a regular restaurant. Not only do you have to worry about the train moving, but also, it obviously does not travel in a straight line—so un-Riga-like! When pouring coffee, you have to be extra careful so that it actually goes into the cup and not onto the table. It took a lot of effort to learn everything, especially given a small kitchen with no dishwasher. Committed to my craft, I never missed a day of work, even in the winter.

No words can properly explain how amazing this experience was and how many fond memories I have of my time on the Orient

Express. Sometimes we served the royal families from Norway, Holland, England, Sweden, Belgium, and Spain. The Royal Family car was separated from the rest of the train, as it was high-class. We would always serve the regular passengers and then close the restaurant to serve the royals.

⁊

One time, Princess (now Queen) Paola of Belgium was traveling with her son, Philippe, who was a year old. One morning, as we served her breakfast, I said to her, "Princess, would you allow me to hold the future king in my arms?"

She then handed him to me, and he peed on the only jacket I had!

"How is it to have royal pee on your jacket?" she asked, smiling.

Serving the royal families involved formal etiquette, exacerbated by the strange quirks each had. If the queen doesn't eat, then no one can eat. The king of Holland (The Netherlands) would carry a bell and shake it each time before he spoke. One time I went to look for the king of Siam (now Thailand), Bhumibol Adulyade, and couldn't find him. He was on the floor playing cards.

A lot of diplomats in Geneva would go to Lugano to fly from its big airport. In the winter, the dining room was full of movie stars, princesses, and kings, who used to go skiing in the Swiss Alps. Sometimes we had two to three hundred special guests and had to serve them all. Sometimes we would run out of bread, and I would have to buy more. If I missed the train upon returning, I had to take another train to meet up with these guests.

The dining room on the Express had forty-eight seats, and they were usually at full capacity. Breakfast was served in fifty-minute shifts. I never let that deter me. They used to call me Speedy Gonzales; I was that fast.

One day, we stopped in Lucerne, Switzerland, and picked up Charlie Chaplin. After I imitated him, he said, "You have a lot of talent, young man. If you want to work on a movie, I can get you there." It takes balls to imitate a movie star like Charlie Chaplin. But I did.

One time, after we entered a tunnel in Lugano, an avalanche hit. We were stuck in the snow for days. We finished all the food we had, and people started panicking. We had no food or water, not even for the bathroom. It smelled rotten. Eventually, they cleared the snow away and dug out the train. We were free.

The Orient Express provided me with a great opportunity to meet people and do what I love: feed people. One time, I had to serve two hundred guests. Nobody came to work due to the snow, so it was on me to make all the guests our standard continental breakfast. With no cooks or waiters, just my dishwasher and me, I served two hundred people in eighty minutes. I explained to them that I was by myself. I made about $500 in tips that day. In all my successes, I have given credit to God, because with God, all things are possible. I could not have done that without Him.

One day, while working, I met a beautiful lady named Carla, a divorcée. I told my mother that I was going to marry her. In response, my mother trekked all the way to Switzerland. She beat me with a broom and stressed that you do not marry divorced women.

In 1963, when I was twenty-five, I left Switzerland to go to England for more exciting opportunities. Carla was heartbroken and begged me not to go. Six months later, I came back to Switzerland for a visit. I told Carla that I wanted more for my life and was going to stay in England. Something deep inside me told me to keep going. My instincts had kept me on the right path so far, so I had to press on. Carla offered to buy me my own hotel or a Mercedes if I stayed. But in my mind, it was wrong to marry a divorced woman. This was what we were taught in Catholic school, and I had quite literally had my mother beat it into me. It was time for us to part ways.

You know, I never looked for a job in my life. Even when I went to England, I had a job waiting for me. I was blessed with connections that directed my course. After residing in England, I was officially able to speak five languages: Italian, French, German, Spanish, and English. I felt strong, educated, and confident as I headed toward the next destination God had in store for me.

※

Julie's Reflections

When people ask me how I was raised, meaning what religion, I always say I was raised "confused." I had a passionate, crazy, amazing Italian father and a logical, money-saving, tennis-playing, Jewish mother who stayed home to raise us. And yes, she did cook. Dad was not home much. The restaurant business takes so much of your time.

I have a few memories of when I was very young. One is still hearing Hall and Oates on the radio (or maybe my parents had the album), but for some reason, I can remember the songs from when I was so small, maybe even four years old. We lived in Edison, New Jersey, and had the best neighbors ever, with whom we are still friends. Around this time, I believe Dad had the restaurant in East Orange, and we would go there often. I do remember sitting on the floor with a blanket and seeing my dad's face on television. Back then, we did not have a way to tape TV shows, but I knew it was Dad on TV.

A few years later we moved to Livingston, New Jersey. I was five years old and that is where I experienced most of my memories. Sunday was always family day, when Dad cooked. It was the only day I saw him for a short time. Most Sundays he spent cooking, watching soccer, and working in the garden. He would also make time to eat with us. It was always a feast with the best food.

⚘

Leadership Lesson 2:
Creativity, Confidence, and Courage

Creativity

You only get one chance at life. Have passion! Just be excited at all of the possibilities that are around you. *Create something!* Create a career, a family, a product, a book—anything. You have one life to live; do it up. Find a career you *love*. Not just like or tolerate. If you do this, you will never work a day in your life. You will also almost never be late for work. If you love what you do, you will not mind going the extra mile. You will do quality work. Work hard and smart. No one is going to hand you anything in this world. The harder you work, the luckier you get. Hard work and dedication always pay off.

Love your family and provide for them. Work hard to provide them with the opportunities you never had. Avoid family problems when you can, and do things to help people get along. You do not choose your family; you're stuck with them, and everyone has a different color to his or her personality. Just try (and sometimes you'll have to try really hard) to love your family in spite of themselves. We are all on a learning journey. You are going to need to forgive people for being nasty, and then move on. We all have bad days, and for some reason, we are even nastier with our family members.

Confidence

You are beautiful inside and out, and you have the confidence to conquer the world by faith. Believe in God. Believe you are worthy of all good things. You are skilled, beautiful, level-headed, and yes, likeable. You will only go as far as you believe you can go. Picture what you want and create it in your mind, and then believe it will happen. Dream, and create your course. Do it with your dad, coach, or friend. Search after God and let him lead you. Also, get someone to validate you and your dream. If you cannot believe it yourself, find someone to tell you how great you are. Let them tell you until you believe it; until you are confident in your heart and spirit. Let others help you if you are struggling. Remember, it takes a village to raise a child, and you are not here alone. Reach out and get what you need so that you may cultivate your confidence.

You are fearfully and wonderfully made, and God loves you. You are amazing, smart, talented, and creative. Say it! *I am creative, talented, brilliant, and attractive as well.* Say it until it imprints on your heart. You will need this confidence to take big steps into big shoes.

Courage

Confidence will give you the courage to go after your dreams. It takes courage to create something, to put yourself out there. You need confidence and courage, because resistance will come in so many different forms and try to take you off your course. Something may come at you as criticism or roadblocks. Go forward. The world may fall down on you, but stay on course. You can't let anything get in your way. Pray and pray. Brush it off and keep going forward. Stay on course.

Chef Table Dinners from Ennio's Notebook
Menu 2

~ Antipasti ~
Conchiglie De Vesse

Bay scallops poached tender in white wine and garlic, drizzled with extra-virgin olive oil and a squeeze of lemon and lime, and tossed with fresh chopped herbs.

Served chilled with slices of fresh semolina bread.

~ Insalata ~
Portobella alla Griglia

Portabella mushroom cap brushed with seasoned extra-virgin olive oil and grilled until tender, sliced and served atop balsamic Dijon vinaigrette-laced baby greens finished with shaved Asiago cheese.

~ Entrée ~
Fettuccini con Pesto alla Friuli

A hearty sauce of fresh-diced, sun-dried tomatoes, roasted red peppers and garlic steeped in chicken stock, pesto and extra-virgin olive oil, tossed with fettuccini pasta and finished with a sprinkling of roasted pine nuts and Parmesan cheese.

Menu 2

CONCHIGLIE DE VESSE
(appetizer; serves 4)

Ingredients:

1 pound	Bay scallops
1 tsp.	Fresh garlic (chopped)
2 ounces	Extra-virgin olive oil
2 ounces	White wine
1 ounce	Lime juice
½ ounces	Lemon juice
1 tablespoon	Chopped basil leaves
1 tablespoon	Chopped dill
1 tablespoon	Chopped flat-leaf Italian parsley
To taste	Salt and pepper
4 each	Lemon wedges
1 each	Crusty semolina bread

Preparation:

- Heat a large sauté pan on medium/high heat. Add olive oil and lightly sauté garlic in pan. Add bay scallops and quickly sauté, then add the wine. Bring the wine to a simmer and remove from heat. Try to only cook the scallops about halfway.
- Remove from heat and place scallops in a bowl.

- Add lime juice, lemon juice, chopped basil, dill, parsley, and salt and pepper. Mix thoroughly, cover, and place in refrigerator for several hours or overnight.
- Plate into equal portions, garnish with lemon wedge, and serve with a few slices of semolina bread.

PORTOBELLO ALLA GRIGLIA
(insalata; serves 4)

Ingredients:

4 each	Portobello mushroom caps
12 ounces	Baby greens
4 tablespoons	Asiago cheese (shaved)
¾ cup	Extra-virgin olive oil
¼ cup	Balsamic vinegar
1 teaspoon	Dijon mustard
To taste	Salt and black pepper

Preparation:

- In a bowl, place olive oil, balsamic vinegar, Dijon mustard, and salt and pepper. Whisk together until blended.
- Put the portobello mushrooms on a plate with the gill sides up and brush liberally with the vinaigrette. Let stand for about ten minutes while you heat the grill.
- Grill the portobello mushroom caps for about five to seven minutes on each side and remove from grill.
- Place baby greens in a large salad bowl and add vinaigrette to taste.
- Place equal amounts of greens on four plates.
- While still warm, slice portobello mushrooms into strips and serve one mushroom cap per plate on top of the dressed greens. Top with shaved Asiago cheese and serve.

(Goes well with crusty French bread.)

Asiago Cheese is an Italian cow's milk cheese typical of two specific regions in the north of Italy: Veneto, specifically, and Trentino-Alto Adige. Since the sixteenth century, the tradition of raising cattle led to production of this specific cheese type. Its texture depends on the aging—three-month-old cheese is solidified but quite soft and smooth; eighteen-month-old cheese is very similar to Parmesan; thus, use in recipes varies according to its age.

Fettuccine Con Pesto alla Friuli
(serves 4)

Ingredients:

1 pound	Fettuccine (uncooked fettuccini)
1 tbs.	Garlic (chopped)
3 ounces	Extra-virgin olive oil
8 ounces	Chicken stock
8 ounces	Chopped plum tomatoes
2 tablespoons	Pesto (or chopped fresh basil)
2 tbs.	Sun-dried tomatoes (julienne)
2 tablespoons	Roasted red peppers (diced)
2 tablespoons	Roasted pine nuts
2 tablespoons	Chopped parsley
1 cup	Grated Parmesan cheese
To taste	Salt and pepper

Preparation:

- Put on a pot of salted boiling water to cook pasta.
- Heat a large sauté pan on medium/high heat. Add olive oil and lightly sauté garlic in pan. Add the chopped plum tomatoes, bring to a simmer, and cook for about five minutes. Add chicken stock, salt, and pepper; bring to a simmer; and cook for another five minutes.
- While the mixture simmers, cook pasta to al dente, strain, and then add hot pasta to the tomato and chicken stock

mixture. Reserve some of the pasta water to moisten the pasta if necessary.

- Add sun-dried tomatoes, roasted peppers, pesto, or chopped basil leaves; toss and simmer for a couple of minutes.
- Plate into equal portions and garnish with pine nuts plus parsley; top with grated Parmesan cheese.

CHAPTER 3

— ✆ —

England: 1962 – 1965

THE NEXT STOP was England. This seemed like a natural next step for me, but it was my ultimate desire to live in America, the home of the brave and free. In my eyes, America was the land of opportunities, the place where dreams come true. During World War II, I spent time with the American soldiers. Some of them became my friends, and I visited them every day. This helped me to break up the gloom and doom that was upon us during that time. The soldiers would feed me Spam and treat me like their mascot. Their hope was contagious, and I wanted to be just like them one day. I would sit with them and soak in their conversation as they lounged around—they were all so much older, braver, and from a whole other world.

"What do you want to be when you grow up?" a sergeant once asked me.

"I want to go to America, because you are my heroes," I replied.

✆

THE IMPERIAL HOTEL VICTORIA HOTEL (TURNKEY, ENGLAND, 1962 – 1963)

A major reason I went to England was to learn English. In Europe, if you want to succeed in the hospitality business, you have to speak at least five languages. I was going to immerse myself in it and master it. As I said, I already spoke Italian, French, German, and Spanish. I only hoped that learning English fluently would be my ticket to America.

One afternoon, I received a call from a friend of mine, Davon, who was the maître d'hôtel for the Imperial Hotel. He invited me to go work there as the wine captain. This was an important position: I was head of the waiters and interacted the most with the guests. This required an outgoing personality, as well as maintaining a certain image for the Imperial. I took it very seriously, and I enjoyed interacting with the people.

One night, we held a large banquet for four hundred people. The guests were all lords from London, along with the British royal family. They put me in charge of the top table that held eight people. It was the principal table, right in the center, where Queen Elizabeth was seated. She loved the duck flambé with cherry sauce. We had eight waiters serving with the utmost perfection that night.

We walked out with the flambé. It was always a special part of the meal. My flambé had extra cognac, and occasionally the flame grew so large that it engulfed my face. On the night we were hosting the royal family, I was horrified as the flame covered my face. The next thing I knew, my hair was singed and flames burned my arm. I couldn't turn back at this point, because we were serving royalty. I was in excruciating pain as I tried to push forward. Every part of me was so hot, with the flambé still flaming. As I was serving the Queen Mother, she glanced at my appearance.

"Are you hurt, son?"

"Yes, Your Majesty," I replied.

"Drop it," she said.

"But I have to serve the people," I said.

"Just drop it; you are in pain," she said again. I dropped the flambé on the floor and then rushed into the kitchen to put something on my arm for the burn.

"What did you do?" the chef yelled. Enraged, he started to chase me with a knife.

"Are you going to kill me?" I yelled. I picked up a knife to protect myself. Another chef came in between us, and we dropped our knives, breathing heavily. Infuriated, I marched out of the hotel.

The next day, I went back to work. It soon became just as hellish as the previous day. I had to serve a customer who was giving me a very hard time.

"These eggs, they are not cooked right," he stated. I brought him a new dish, and again, he said they were not cooked right, and sent them back to the kitchen. He sent the eggs back about twenty times before I lost my temper. I brought the final dish toward him and stood next to him as he tasted the eggs. My face was red with annoyance.

"No, not good," he said. He handed the plate back to me and stared at me.

"Not good," he repeated.

My frustration took over. Without really thinking too much further, I dumped the plate all over his lap.

And then I quit.

After what had happened with the Queen Mother, I could only take so much more.

As I was walking back home to my apartment, a friend stopped to tell me that work was available at the Victoria Hotel across the

street. I took this as a sign from God and hurried home to shower. I immediately went over to the Victoria Hotel to see what they were offering. I walked in confidently and greeted management. They hired me on the spot. It was like they were simply waiting for me to quit the Imperial Hotel and come to them.

I knew then that my impulsive decision to leave had been the right thing to do. I was starting to believe that if you are really good at your job, you do not have to worry about getting another one. I would suggest, however, that you not drop eggs on a customer's lap! My motto is that the customer is always right, and when I was young, I didn't have much patience, like most young people. I made many mistakes, but somehow all of my mistakes led me to create a beautiful life. All I had to do was remain true to myself, stay on course, and trust God.

At the Victoria Hotel, it was standard to have a maître d'hôtel and an assistant maître d'hôtel (who also went by the title of wine steward) on staff. I was hired as their wine steward—a great opportunity for me to advance, as well as bring what I had learned as a wine captain from the Imperial Hotel. I was happy to have another chance, but I did not forget what had just gone so terribly wrong at the Imperial.

One afternoon, we had a party comprised of people from London, all formally dressed—the elite of the elite. Out of the entire party, one man was not dressed appropriately. I called in the maître d'hôtel right away.

"This man does not fit into this crowd. I am worried that he snuck in. He's not dressed appropriately at all," I said. He was in jeans and looked messy. How could I have this at the Victoria Hotel?

"Get him and throw him out, now!" the maître d'hôtel demanded. I marched back into the dining area and threw him out of the hotel. A few minutes later, a crowd of angry people gathered outside of the hotel, throwing rocks at the window.

The messy man I had thrown out was Mick Jagger. I had no idea he was just then coming into his own as a rising rock star.

∽

THE RMS *QUEEN ELIZABETH* (1963 – 1965)

A friend of mine invited me to work on the RMS *Queen Elizabeth* as the waiter's chef. This was another great chance to learn from Europe's best chefs, who worked together on this famous ship.

They put me in charge of the International Children and Kosher food. One day, we served an all-kosher breakfast for the Jewish people on board. Somehow, the milk and meat silverware got combined. The guests found out and were furious. The next day, I threw all the silverware into the ocean, and from then on, served kosher food with plastic silverware only. This eliminated confusion and kept my Jewish friends happy.

Working on the ship was hard work and stressful on the body. We made long journeys and had tight quarters. Every seven days, the RMS *Queen Elizabeth* crossed the ocean. We went back and forth to the same ports, with the exception of the forty-day cruise. I made a lifetime friend who I loved dearly, Franco, on the RMS *Queen Elizabeth* and met plenty of celebrities. Many times, the news would report about who would be on the ship, and we would find out before they arrived. In 1964, we had Elizabeth Taylor and Richard Burton as guests. Elizabeth Taylor was one of the biggest movie stars then, so she created quite the buzz. We also had Debbie Reynolds and Eddie Fisher, plus one of my favorites, Connie Stevens, as a guest. What a nice woman she was to serve. All of the rich and royals traveled on the RMS *Queen Elizabeth*. It was a glorious ship with beautiful art and a romantic flair. The food was also top-notch, of course.

My dear friend Franco and I had many dangerous adventures. Some crewmembers were nasty, and you really had to watch yourself. One day, Franco went to the kitchen and ordered four chickens for lunch.

A chef gave him a chicken kidney instead. Franco eyed it and said, "No, sir, I ordered chickens."

The chef responded by throwing the kidney in Franco's face, causing him to duck and turn red.

"Franco, go change for work," I said, stepping toward them, trying to put some distance between the two. The chef came closer toward me, trying to get to Franco. I looked at the chef in bewilderment.

"Why would you do that to Franco?" I asked him. The chef picked up the casserole on the table next to us and threw it at my face. My arm swung to punch him right in the face, and the next thing I knew we were fighting. A few waiters and some of the other chefs in the kitchen had to pull us apart.

When we stood in front of the captain to explain our tussle, I explained what happened honestly. The chef was fired without pay. After that, nobody on the ship messed with me. They knew better. In life, you must defend yourself and your friends from harm. In life, you must survive tough situations; having faith in

God and the power He gives you will get you through the toughest times. You must stay true to yourself and stay on course.

Although I worked hard and enjoyed my work, I was still in search of true love. I dreamed that one day I would have a family of my own. On one warm day, a beautiful young lady and her grandmother were boarding for the forty-day cruise. Judie and her grandmother, Mildred, became two guests I saw frequently. In time, Judie fell in love with me. Perhaps it was because I had cooked tableside for them for forty days and nights. We did share some nice moments together.

During their time aboard, and after we said our goodbyes, I received a letter from Judie asking me if I wanted to come to America and get married. This was the chance I was waiting for: the chance to go to America. I thought about it for a while and knew it was a risk to leave the ship. My dreams took over, however, and I took a chance that would change my life forever. I resigned from the RMS *Queen Elizabeth* and set out to follow Judie to America.

Leadership Lesson 3:
P.R.E.S.E.N.C.E.

My father was the embodiment of hospitality and service; he "showed up" in a way that was engaging and compelling. To this day, people remember his presence.

PRESENCE =
Passion, Realness, Entrance, Service, Niceness, Confidence, Excellence

Passion

> *Look at this, Julie: I live in paradise.*
> *—Chef Riga*

Wherever my dad lived, he was in awe of the beautiful land and cherished the gardens, trees, and sunlight. He taught me that life is beautiful, and we have so much to cherish and be thankful for. I learned to rise above hard times and stay on course. Most importantly, I learned to have a *passion* for life.

We only get one chance at this, and you might as well live the best life you can. Apply your passion for life to everything you do. If you cook, do it with passion and love. If you have a soul mate, love with passion. If you teach or raise children, do it with passion and care. People are drawn to you when you are passionate about something. It helps them believe—and get excited about—what is possible. If you love what you do, you will never work a day in your life.

How do you keep your passion in hard times? I've certainly had my fair share.

Passion means having a strong emotion. For Christians, it also means the suffering and death of Jesus Christ. (Note: If spirituality is not your thing, you can skip down to the Realness section).

God the father had so much passion for us that the word used for the crucifixion of Messiah Jesus literally is *passion* (from late Latin, *passionem*, meaning "suffering, enduring," and/or *patior* or *passio*, meaning "suffer"; its first recorded use is in early Latin translations of the Bible that appeared in the second century A.D. and described Jesus's death). In John 3:16, the Bible says, "For God so loved the world, He gave his only Son, so that whoever believes in Him shall not perish, but have eternal life." When we believe that God sent His son as the last final sacrifice required in the Jewish Law, we embody that passion by inviting the Holy Spirit to live in us. In the Old Testament, God was always looking for a dwelling place. When we open our hearts to God, we open a space for life-passion, through which all things are possible.

This passion becomes contagious; people can see it. The Holy Spirit gives us a passion for life that transcends this life into heaven.

Passion looks a whole lot different with God in its midst. In John 16:33, the Bible says: "I have told you these things, so that in me, you may have peace. In this world, you will have trouble. But take heart! I have overcome the world." Matthew 19:26 says, "With man this is impossible, but with God all things are possible." For those of you who do not believe, pause and consider—and if you have lost your belief, perhaps reconsider. Based on my own experience, your level of passion will rise the closer you get to God. So why not have passion?

Realness

We are like raindrops; you can see right through us.
—Chef Riga

You establish trust through genuine interactions. Being real is the birthplace of connection—and discovering who you are is where you start.

So many experiences allow us to discover ourselves, but the most targeted way I recommend is to complete a Myers-Briggs Type Indicator Step II personality assessment, and then use it to create your personal mission statement.

As a coach and trainer, I have worked with people on life-changing self-discovery sessions. To grow and get the most out of life, we need to consistently learn and develop. Spending time in reflection allows us to have the courage to own that story and be authentic.

Once you truly discover yourself, be proud of your story. Owning the story of who you are is exciting. Being proud of who you are will allow you to be compellingly real, it will give you the *charisma* (from the Greek word *kharisma*, from *kharis*, "favor, grace" from God) to create a memorable presence.

Entrance

*If the world falls down on your shoulders, brush it off and
stay on course; don't look back.*
—Chef Riga

Check in with yourself. Before you enter a room, ask: How am I feeling right now? Am I tapping into my passion and able to be real? Do I know how I want to show up to the person with whom I am about to speak? Can I hone in on that person's needs, and how I can provide a service? And finally, am I ready to make the person I am speaking with the momentary center of my world? My father made everyone feel like he or she was the most important person in the room. He had an entrance like no other, because he had the hospitality mindset.

Be engaging, even bold. Make eye contact, smile, and enjoy the time you have with this person. Practice and perfect it so that you can enter with grace.

Service

*If you wash dishes, do it with passion; if you cook a meal,
do it with love; and if you manage a restaurant, do it with
excellence, and provide the highest level of service.*
—Chef Riga

Having a service mindset is about realizing what a person's needs are. To find out a need, focus on *listening*, which is connected to how you enter. Enter a room or situation with the mindset that "I am going to listen and be curious about what is going on with that other person, so that I may provide some sort of service."

Service provides us with an experience that goes beyond what we see. If we take the focus off ourselves and put it on the person in front of us, connection happens, because then that person feels like the most important person in the world.

Expertise

Know your product; taste the foods you are trying to sell… Managers and service staff should taste all the daily specials they will be selling.
—Chef Riga

Know whatever it is you're selling. You are providing a service—and customers want to know what you think of the products you are selling. Once you are an expert on your product, you can recommend how to make customers happy. Be as descriptive as possible so that they can actually picture your offering in their heads…and confirm their choice once they make it, so they don't experience "buyer's remorse." Being an expert at your subject matter or products will help your customers trust you.

And by the way...experts get paid! Value is always associated with expertise. So why keep it to yourself?

Niceness

Remember, everyone needs a smile.
—Chef Riga

Hospitality flows from a friendly and generous reception, which means entertaining both known guests and visitors...even strangers. Sharing a warm smile and a positive, friendly attitude will create a great impression. People are drawn to you by your kindness... and kindness will help you create the presence you are seeking.

Character is key. How far can you go simply by being nice? Do the right thing for people—and in God's eyes—and you will go far. Again, having a trustworthy character will speak volumes to your audience. When we fail, we need not beat ourselves up. This can take us off course, when we need to stay on course. Brush it off, apologize, and self-correct for as many times as you fail. As long as you try to be the best version of yourself, you will keep going forward. Do it until you get it right, and don't punish yourself for your failures. Celebrate your successes, however small they may seem at the time.

Respect is the deep admiration we have for someone based on his or her abilities, qualities, position, or achievements. How much value you are placing on a person? It seems easy to be nice or kind to something or someone we value. How well are you valuing your customers, family, team, and God?

Confidence

> I am humble—and a national treasure.
> —Chef Riga

The way we view ourselves dictates how we show up for each of our interactions. Chef Riga never forgot where he came from or the journey he had. Sure, he also knew his gift…and he celebrated it. Although he only had an elementary-school education, his life provided the learning opportunities that helped him succeed. My dad had confidence that he could accomplish anything.

Confidence comes from a deep sense of knowing who you are and what your strengths are. It helps if you have people around you who love and support you. My father helped instill a deep sense of confidence in me by his words, but even more so by his example. I believed that I could have the same level of success as my dad, because I knew what he did to get there.

And yes, while I was privileged to be part of my dad's family, how much more privilege do I enjoy as a child of God? Sure, I derive confidence from my skill, talent, and family—but even more of it comes from having a deep sense of belonging to God's family and knowing that I will see my dad again. I know he is waiting for me and will greet me one day when this journey ends.

Your confidence will create a presence that will allow you to connect.

Excellence

When you cook a meal, do it with passion and excellence.
—Chef Riga

When you flavor your dreams with wonder, excitement, and possibility, you have the ability to take yourself to new heights… and when you explore new heights, you strive for excellence. It speaks to your brilliance, the quality of the product you are providing, and the caliber of person you are.

Setting yourself apart from the rest of the pack sets you up for success. Having time to reflect and study your expertise brings you forward in a way that forges your reputation. When you are known for your reputation, people want you around, because you make everything around you *that much better.* Because you consistently demonstrate excellence, others want you on their team.

Presence = Passion, Realness, Entrance, Service, Niceness, Confidence, Excellence

Chef Table Dinners from Ennio's Notebook
Menu 3

~ Antipasti ~

Cozze Christina

Fresh mussels poached and individually topped with a colorful mixture of marinated, finely diced red and green peppers, tomatoes, and red onion, seasoned with a hint of Dijon mustard and garlic. Served chilled.

~ Insalata ~

Pomodori e Cipolla

Diced fresh mozzarella cheese and roasted red peppers tossed in a pesto balsamic vinaigrette, served over ripe red tomato slices.

~ Entrée ~

Veal Scaloppini alla Riga

Twin veal medallions sautéed and topped with eggplant, prosciutto, and melted Fontina cheese, served with capellini marinara and a generous sprinkling of grated Grana Padano cheese.

Menu 3

Cozze Cristina
(appetizer; serves 4)

Ingredients:

2 dozen	Fresh black mussels
1 teaspoon	Garlic (chopped)
3 ounces	Extra-virgin olive oil
1 each	Green pepper (diced fine)
1 each	Red pepper (diced fine)
1 each	Red onion (diced fine)
1 each	Plum tomato (diced small)
1 teaspoon	Dijon mustard
2 tablespoons	Chopped parsley
2 tablespoons	Chopped fresh basil leaves
1 each	Lemon (squeeze juice from 1 lemon)
1 each	Lemon (cut in quarters for garnish)
3 splashes	Lea & Perrins Worcestershire sauce
To taste	Salt and pepper

Preparation:

- Clean mussels and poach them in water until open. Remove from liquid, discard top half of shell, and chill. (Poaching liquid can be water only, or you can add white wine and some lemon juice.)

- In a large bowl, combine all the other ingredients listed (except for lemon wedges) and chill.
- After all ingredients are cold, top each mussel with mixture.
- Serve six mussels on each plate, with a lemon wedge for garnish.

Pomodori con Cipolla
(insalata; serves 4)

Ingredients:
- 12 each   Ripe tomato slices (½-inch thick)
- 12 ounces   Fresh mozzarella cheese (diced)
- 2 each   Red onion slices (¼-inch thick)
- 4 ounces   Roasted pepper (diced)
- 3 ounces   Extra-virgin olive oil
- 1 ounce   Balsamic vinegar
- 1 tablespoon   Pesto
- To taste   Salt and black pepper

Preparation:

- In a bowl, place olive oil, balsamic vinegar, pesto, and salt and pepper. Whisk together until blended.
- Add diced mozzarella and diced roasted peppers to the pesto vinaigrette and toss together.
- Cut tomato slices in half, and on each plate, arrange six tomato half slices circularly, ringing the plate center.
- Place equal amounts of mozzarella and roasted pepper mixture in the center of the ringed tomatoes.
- Break the onion slices into individual rings and place several rings on top of each plate as garnish.
- Serve chilled.

Veal Scaloppine alla Riga
(serves 4)

Ingredients:

1 pound (8 2-ounce pieces)	Veal medallions (sliced, pounded thin)
8 slices	Eggplant (¼-inch thick round slices)
8 slices	Prosciutto
8 slices	Fontina cheese
3 ounces	Extra-virgin olive oil
10 ounces	Marinara sauce (homemade or good quality)
2 to 3 ounces	Grana Padano (grated)
12 ounces	Capellini pasta (cooked al dente)
1 tablespoon	Chopped parsley

Preparation:

- Preheat oven to 400°. Also preheat large sauté pan on medium/high flame and add 1.5 ounces olive oil. Sauté the eggplant slices and put aside.
- Leave sauté pan on the heat, add remaining olive oil, and sauté veal medallions until they have a little brown color to them.
- When veal is cooked, turn down heat and add 4 ounces marinara sauce to warm the sauce.

- On a small sheet pan or large heatproof platter, coat the bottom with the heated marinara sauce and build individual stacks: one slice each of veal, topped with eggplant, then prosciutto and Fontina cheese. Place the pan in the oven until the Fontina cheese is melted.
- While the scaloppini stacks are in the oven, use your same sauté pan and heat the remaining marinara sauce. Reheat the capellini in the pan, along with the marinara sauce.
- Once the veal medallion stacks are heated through and cheese melted, serve two stacks on each plate, with 3 ounces capellini.
- Top with grated Grana Padano and parsley.

This dish also goes well with polenta, a dish of boiled cornmeal typical of Northern Italian regions.

Scaloppine come in many variations: the thinly sliced meat (covered in a little wheat flour and sautéed) is then served with several different sauces; including tomato, lemon, mushroom, white wine, etc.

Fontina cheese is another Italian cow's milk cheese. It is a typical product of the Aosta Valley, a northern Italian region surrounded by Piedmont, Switzerland, and France. Its flavor can vary from intense to milder options. It is often used to cook fondue (melted cheese dip).

CHAPTER 4

—— ⚘ ——

America: Part I, 1965 – 1976

I FINALLY VENTURED to the United States after a long trip over the Atlantic. I was determined to accomplish my dreams.

Judie and I, unfortunately, ended rather soon after my arrival. I caught her making love with another man and was devastated. I had come all the way from Italy to marry this woman, just to see her betray me. I couldn't compete with that. I called Mildred, her grandmother, who came to pick me up.

As I was leaving, I told Judie, "May you suffer like me."

After ending things with Judie, I spent the rest of the summer in Detroit Lake with Mildred. She was amazing, and I was always indebted to her for everything she did for me. When the summer ended, I went back to Cleveland. Mildred's husband, Clinton, fell ill and was sent to the hospital. I spent most days with him. Clinton was a wonderful man. Before he got sick, he had been a fundraiser for colleges.

I became close with the family; I owed them for my ability to stay in the United States, and in turn, I took care of them. They were like second parents to me. As Clinton was dying—of cancer, I believe—I spent most of my time taking care of him. Later, he died in my arms.

Clinton had intended to leave me money and his wealth. Because nothing was ever formally written down, however, Judie and his other children protested, and I received nothing. While I was extremely frustrated, I was sure karma would handle it...and I was indebted for how greatly the family had affected my life, regardless.

Mildred knew a congresswoman who told her of a restaurant that was very popular with members of Congress. I decided to work there for free to obtain my green card. I served Robert F. Kennedy and other senators. Mildred spoke highly of me, telling the restaurant, "This young man works hard. I promised him that I would help him stay in this country, so please help him. He's very talented." These senators helped grant me permission to stay in this country. I was very fortunate and blessed. Mr. Kennedy ended up helping me obtain my green card.

surgeon, was soon not enough. He added music, choreography, knife- and fruit-tossing. He was soon hired at Cleveland's City Club, a members-only eatery for the politically connected.

He says that Robert F. Kennedy, on seeing Riga peel a pineapple in a single, snake-like section, then slice it with a knife tossed in midair and caught, on the downbeat, between choruses of Louis Prima's "Buona Sera, Signorina," was at first speechless. Riga says he took a deep bow, then later informed him that his visa was almost up. Kennedy pulled strings, and Riga got a green card from the Immigration and Naturalization Service, enabling him to remain and work in the United States.

Throughout this time, I had no money, but after getting my green card, I was able to find a job at the 13 Colony Hotel as the metro hotel manager. Shortly thereafter, they promoted me to assistant manager. It was a very beautiful place.

One day, a comedian at the club asked me to make him pasta. He said, "Ennio, what are you doing here? You belong in New York. I'm going to tell them how talented you are with your flambé and tell them to hire you." A week later, I got an appointment for an interview.

After much consideration, Mildred paid for my flight to New York. Upon my arrival, I met up with a few men the comedian connected me with and traveled to a famous restaurant, where ten people awaited me in the kitchen.

The man who brought me simply said, "Cook for them."

In front of me were all the ingredients I needed to cook, as well as complete access to the magnificent kitchen before me.

Before I even finished the Steak Diablo, I was told I would be the next special chef at the Peacock Alley in the Waldorf-Astoria.

ცੈ

THE WALDORF-ASTORIA (NEW YORK CITY, 1968–1972)

The Waldorf-Astoria's Peacock Alley was then one of the most famous restaurants in America—a five-star establishment located inside the hotel. I was cooking tableside, as was my specialty and signature style. I was in charge of cooking for our special guests. I would engage and entertain the high-end guests as they ate delicacies. My salary was higher than the hotel manager's.

Everybody who was famous stayed at the Waldorf and ate at Peacock Alley. All types of personalities graced our tables.

This included one of the greatest football coaches of all time, Vince Lombardi.

One time, he asked me, "Ennio, would you dance with my wife?"

"Okay, Mr. Lombardi, I will dance with your wife." I took Mrs. Lombardi's hand, and we had a grand old time dancing. We took a picture together, Mr. Lombardi and I, and I asked him if he would sign it.

"No, you do it. This will be a great gift for my wife," Mr. Lombardi said. So I signed it. That was the last time I ever saw him. Vince Lombardi passed away on September 3, 1970. What a great man he was! I was very sad to hear about his death.

❧

Throughout this time, I often cooked for other famous and influential people. The Mafia held lots of power during this time, and the infamous crime families frequented Peacock Alley regularly. I also had the pleasure to cook for Golda Meir, the prime minister of Israel. What a wonderful lady! She spoke several languages. I took her to the suites and she asked me to take care of her food, especially because she was, of course, Kosher. Besides Golda Meir, we had many presidents and world leaders stay at the Waldorf. King Hussein would occasionally stay as well. One time, he asked me to cook brunch for him. I had to tell him I was unable to, because I had to make it to the airport to leave for Italy. King Hussein asked me to still make brunch for him and, in return, had a helicopter take me to the airport so I would not miss my flight. Incredible.

The Waldorf-Astoria

CONRAD N. HILTON CHAIRMAN

Office of the Manager

April 28, 1971

Mr. Ennio Riga
The Ground Floor
CBS Building
New York, N. Y.

Dear Ennio:

In the months since you left the Waldorf-Astoria, your many
friends, fans and co-workers have thought of you often and
missed you a great deal. When you came to us two years ago,
you also brought a number of interesting sidelights. The most
obvious, of course, was your talent for gourmet cooking, which
many people sampled with delight. Your most unusual bit of
flavor, however, had nothing to do with cooking spices. To
watch your smiling face and dancing feet while your talented
hands rythmically chopped, seasoned and musically prepared
your many unique epicurean delights was, indeed, a very special
treat for many people. You most certainly earned the right
to be called our Terpsichorean Epicure, for you cooked and danced
your way into the hearts of a great many Waldorf-Astoria guests.

Even though we were sad to see you leave us, we know your
decision was made wisely, to further your career and discover
more about your abilities. We hope you will reflect back upon
your years at the Waldorf-Astoria with a smile, while you
simultaneously look forward to a brilliant future filled with
star-studded accomplishments.

You have our sincere wishes for all of the good things life has
to offer. You deserve the very best.

Kindest regards,

Frank Arthur Banks
Vice President and Manager

The attention I was getting as a chef landed me spots on television programs in the United States: Johnny Carson, Dick Cavett, Mike Douglas, *Good Morning America, To Tell the Truth,* and Joe Franklin, to name a few. I even had my own cooking show. Everyone was so nervous when I was on the Johnny Carson show. I cut myself and I was bleeding like a pig, but I finished the show anyway. It was a success, thrill, and honor to be on his show. I had reviews written about me and was featured in newspaper and magazine stories all over the country. I was the number one chef in America for cooking tableside. My guests were endless—royalty, movie stars, politicians…and in the end, let me tell you: everyone is the same. They all want to feel welcome, and they all want to eat well.

Peacock Alley was the place to work. I had so many amazing experiences working there that I would not have had anywhere else. I will always remember that on certain weekends, the Kennedys would send a plane for me. I would be taken to Martha's Vineyard and cook for them tableside privately.

From what I witnessed, I also began to conclude that show business, even with its glamour, could be a very cruel and lonely world. All of these millionaires were so depressed and lonely. At one point, I met (Władziu Valentino) Liberace at the Waldorf. He would wear the most beautiful mink coat. He always ate very light—a little salad, and no garlic. I also made a risotto alla Milanese with saffron for him that he enjoyed. I was unable to make the fruit flambé for him, because he was in a rush. When

I ran into him years later, he recognized me. We began to talk, and I felt as though he was no longer the same man. He seemed very depressed. We spoke about his piano, and he told me the piano itself cost him half a million dollars. All of this money, and yet he did not seem happy. But let me tell you something: that man could play the piano. He was magnificent. He was one of the greatest piano players I've ever met.

If you think riches will make you happy, I don't think so. I have seen and experienced how the lavish live their lives with their money. I remember how Nelson Rockefeller would never tip more than 10 percent. He never gave an extra tip—not once. What good is it to have that kind of money and not share it with a person who does something for you? That always astounded me. Tell me what good that is.

Bob Hope never left me a great tip, but he was a good man. He was very close with Connie Stevens. He would give her money for the children when money was tight.

I was fortunate enough to meet Connie while she was married to Eddie Fisher. Eddie would come to me and ask to borrow five dollars. I would give it to him. Connie would beg me, "Ennio, please don't give him any more money. He wanted it for drinks. I cannot take it anymore. He is an alcoholic and a drug addict." I could not understand how a woman, any woman, could go for a man like that.

Liza Minnelli and I used to go out to different restaurants in the city together. We used to go to a small Greek place in Manhattan. One night, she got so sick from drinking this red wine that I had to take her back to my place and let her stay there.

We used to have nuns come to the Waldorf occasionally. One time, they gave me a certificate to heaven, if I kept the command-ments. I don't know if I have kept the commandments, but I do like to help people. It feels good. Everybody has a conscience and a soul. Doing something good for people is good for the soul—so all of you should do something good. If you are rich, help others. I remember on one occasion in New York, I was on my way home around midnight, and I saw three guys beating up a homeless man. I went to fight these men. I must have looked like an animal, because the guys ran away. Another time, I saw a guy bleeding on the street. I knocked on people's doors but nobody came to help; in fact, the people from one of the houses called the police on me. I was going to get arrested for trying to help a man. The police ar-rived and said that people had filed a complaint against me. I said I was trying to get help for the man who was hurt. He would die from bleeding in a few minutes if nobody helped him. The police said to me, *that's the way it is.* They then let me go.

When I worked at the Waldorf, I had so many offers to become partners with Sirio, the owner of the most famous restaurant in the world. I was not, however, ready to become second fiddle to anybody. When the opportunity came for me to be in charge of a restaurant on the Caribbean island of St. Martin, however, I took it.

⚘

Flambé
The Dancing Chef

Choose a selection of your favorite fruit cut up while singing and dancing to your favorite song or the El Cumbanchero.

- Melon
- Apples
- Bananas
- Strawberries
- Raspberry
- Grapes

Things are really swinging these days at the Waldorf-Astoria's Peacock Alley. Ennio Riga, a superb gourmet chef and flambé artist, has been busy presenting his flaming specialties. At the same time, he performs a lively samba, tango, or Charleston. Every night except Sunday from 6 P.M. on, Mr. Riga combines his terpsichorean and culinary arts. While the musicians play his special music, Ennio Riga prepares steak Diane, steak Rita, or veal scallopini. For a taste of one of his flambé dishes, make a reservation at Peacock Alley.

DANCING DESSERT

To celebrate a special occasion or to fabricate one out of any ordinary evening, there could scarcely be a treat more flamboyantly festive than Ennio Riga's gourmet performance in Peacock Alley at the Waldorf-Astoria. Imagine this: the lights go down, the music begins, flames lick the sides of the shallow, flat pan on the cart, and the magician in charge begins to dance. While dancing—samba, tango and Charleston—he deftly peels and slices into the pan, a pineapple, a pear, apples, oranges, bananas, and grapes. (Yes, he even peels a couple of grapes.) Brandy and rum go into the mixture, which is flamed, poured over ice cream, and topped with whipped cream. This is the dessert and *pièce de résistance.*

The menu of specialties prepared tableside (for two or more persons) by Ennio includes gourmet dishes for every course, most of them involving wine, brandy and flames—and they are as delicious as they are spectacular. Ennio Riga is a young Venetian who loves to cook, and to talk about cooking. Prices for his creations range from $1.75 for Caesar Salad to $9.25 for sirloin a la Pizzaiola, with the dancing dessert at $2.50. For reservations—beginning at 6 p.m., Monday through Saturday—call 355-3000.

Flambé Sauce
- Sugar
- Butter
- Brandy
- Orange Juice
- Cinnamon

Flame
Once heated, douse it with Rum and Grand Marnier

Serve over vanilla ice cream

79

Island Chalet (Saint Maarten, Netherlands Antilles, 1972 – 1973)

I left America in 1972 to become president of the Island Chalet in St. Martin. They were building a new restaurant to develop tourism. When I arrived, the restaurant wasn't fully built yet. I had to get people together and help actually construct the place. I managed about fifty people.

Life was different in St. Martin, and I had to get used to those differences quickly. One day, one of my drivers went to pick some up some of the day workers and did not see a woman crossing the street. He hit her and tragically, she died from the accident. Two days later, they found my driver hanging by the neck at the accident location. I got the message quickly: that was how things were done here.

One time after my driver was killed, I went to the French side alone. Six or seven black men approached me, and I thought to myself, "Oh God, I'm dead." I said to them, "I'm one-two, I'm one-two—please don't kill me." So instead of killing me, they helped me. They knew I was a good man. After that day, everybody on the island called me One Too. I had a very good reputation on the island.

Prior to moving to St. Martin, I met a woman at the Columbus Club in Manhattan. It was three a.m., and I was accompanied by two others from the premiere of a Lainie Kazan film. I was wearing a tuxedo, and so was my colleague. The Columbus Club was an after-hours place, someplace you could go and grab eggs Benedict and have a grand old time. At that particular time,

Davy Jones from the Monkees was there. They went there to eat. Everybody went there for breakfast. You walked into the club through a grand entrance, then down the stairs to be seated by the maître d'hôtel. It was an elegant breakfast place.

A beautiful young woman was sitting at a table near the grand entrance with two other women when I arrived that night. I would later learn that her name was Rose. She was wearing a Duke University sweatshirt and jeans. And here I was, in a tuxedo. As the maître d'hôtel brought us down the entrance stairs, she looked at me and simply called out, "Hello!"

"Hello!" I smiled at her, surprised. "Nobody says hello like that in the city." I then asked the maître d'hôtel to seat us at the table next to these girls. I pushed the tables together and said, "Breakfast is on me!"

The woman who had come from the premiere with my friend and I ended up knowing Rose's friend at the table, Arlene. They began talking and catching up, and Rose's other friend, Wanda, began talking to my friend. I engaged in conversation with the beautiful woman who had called out to me. We were all having a great time. You see what good food and good company does? None of us got home that evening until about seven a.m.

I gave Rose my business card as we parted and told her I would cook for her. Rose later claimed that when she heard that, I got her attention. I told her to give me a call the next time she came into the city. I promised I would make a reservation for her and cook for her and her friends, Arlene and Wanda, who had an apartment there.

Time passed, and then, out of the blue, I received a call from Rose. She was visiting Arlene and Wanda and taking me up on my offer. I was so happy to hear from her. I sent a cab to their apartment. Once they arrived, I cooked for them, and the four of us spent the whole night together.

After I got off work, we went to a bar and got drinks. Rose claimed that she was not interested in me at first and saw me as a friend, but I won her over with the food and my charm. I would see Rose one or two more times before I took a bus to Irvington, New Jersey, where I met her entire family at a barbeque. I went to the supermarket and bought all kinds of food. I cooked the entire day. Her whole extended family was there, but we were not in a relationship yet. It was already known that I would be leaving soon for the islands...but this did not stop me. I knew I wanted to marry Rose right away. I asked Rose's father for her hand in marriage, and when he said yes, my heart leaped. I knew this was right. I told her to get herself organized, and then I would send for her soon.

After six months of hard labor in St. Martin, I was very lonely. I called Rose and asked her if she would marry me and come to the islands. Rose told me she would need an apartment and a car, and I made that happen for her. I wanted her to be as comfortable as possible. Even so, Rose told me she could not marry me in St. Martin and that I would have to first come home to New Jersey.

Our marriage happened in a whirlwind. We got the blood test, the dress, a full house, a piano player, and a man to marry us for a mixed marriage (as Rose was Jewish and I was Christian)—all within a week. Catering, music, photographer...everything was organized and done so quickly. Rose called everyone on the telephone to invite him or her to the wedding. I believe about fifty people came. It was at the home of Flo, a woman Rose worked for in Hillside, New Jersey, as a hairdresser.

As we cut the cake, I sang to Rose, "More...than the greatest love the world has ever known..." Mildred, the grandmother to whom I was so indebted, came all the way from Cleveland to attend the wedding.

As all of this planning was going on, I packed my bags in St. Martin and traveled back to New Jersey to marry my future wife. I arrived on a Thursday, and we were officially engaged. On Friday, we went to the courthouse and got the marriage license. On Sunday, we were married in front of all of Rose's family and friends, plus Mildred. My family could not come, but they were happy for me. On Monday, I was traveling back to St. Martin to work.

When I arrived, the restaurant was ready. I had a nice apartment near the airport for Rose and me. My staff at the island was truly amazing. I worked side by side with them every day. But as time passed, Rose and I began to feel that it was time to come back to America.

Throughout our stay in St. Martin, Rose helped out and built a life with me. She would drive the natives to work, and she did a lot of errands on behalf of the restaurant and resort. One day, the owner of the place gave Rose a bill for a meal she ate. As my wife, she was supposed to eat for free. She brought it to me and I was infuriated.

I took the check back to the owner and said, "Let me give you a 'tip.'" Then I punched him. I quit on the spot, and Rose and I quickly walked out to the car. All of the natives came running after us, and we started the first strike on the island.

When my employees found out I was leaving, every person in the restaurant and hotel quit working. I said, "I'm in trouble now." From dishwashing to captain, everybody quit. I told them to go back to work. They said they would rather leave to America with me. I told them again that they needed to go back to work. Back at our apartment, I got a call from the restaurant and resort owner. He said if I came back to work with my crew, they would double everyone's salary. So once more, I told my crew to go back to work, hoping they would listen. Two hours later, police cars pulled up to our apartment. They said to me, "We will let you go, but you have to leave this island within twenty-four hours and tell the entire crew to go back to work."

I explained the situation to everybody and asked them go to back to work. I told them that they were going to be paid double, and it was very good money. My crew then agreed to go back to work. I was lucky that I wasn't sent to jail. The owner was infuriated that my quitting had created this chaos for the restaurant.

When Rose and I were leaving to head home to America, my entire crew and staff were there to say goodbye to me. While I left the island feeling good about myself, and happy that I had a wife, I was sad to leave my staff behind. They were like my children. I was only thirty-three but felt I had so much life experience and cared so much for them. I worked with them side by side throughout the whole construction phase. We made a rock wall, put down grass, and worked in the restaurant. We built that restaurant from the ground up. It was our home. We were a family. That said, knowing that all my workers were going to be okay helped me leave in peace. They would be working for another company, would make more money, and would (hopefully) be treated better.

When you have circumstances like that, help people the best you can. Stay on course, and help others stay on course as well. Make them feel like they have dignity, and you'll feel rewarded. Teach with your heart—passion, faith, and love—and you will be okay. The reward is incredible.

Being a chef sometimes means you have to work with pain, with cuts, and still finish the job. It can be done! But as in any part of life, if you're not able to work with pain, you will never make it.

✁

THE SKYLINE HOTEL (NEW YORK CITY, 1974 – 1976)

When we first returned to America, we stayed with Rose's parents. I worked in a catering hall and a pizzeria to make ends meet, while Rose was pregnant with our daughter, Julie. We contemplated moving to Florida, but hotel executive Rudy Mazzonelli then offered me a position at the Skyline Inn Hotel in 1974. You never know where life's next opportunity will come from. I had shared an apartment with him on Fifty-sixth and Lexington in New York before he got married and I moved to Sutton Place. My neighbor then was Julie Newmar, better known as "Catwoman." Sometimes she would let me ride her bicycle. I used to pay $650 in rent in the 1970s. In today's money, that's about $3,000 a month. They paid me very well—about $700 a week. I used to drive a red Fiat to work. Rose and I lived a very comfortable life.

The trial of former attorney general John N. Mitchell was underway in spring 1974. Mitchell was being charged with obstructing a federal investigation in the Watergate scandal. He would later be convicted and serve a sentence for conspiracy, obstruction of justice, and lying under oath. The jury for his hearing was sequestered for six months at the Skyline Inn. They couldn't communicate with their families or watch television. They were going crazy! I tried to make them feel comfortable by cooking tableside and making different styles of foods for them: Italian, French, anything to entertain them and make them feel better. Each morning, I would make their breakfast, and then they would get in a bus and leave for the courthouse. Each night, they would come back to the hotel, exhausted. By the end of the trial, only thirteen jurors remained.

Leadership Lesson 4:
Chef Riga's Leadership Lessons Are a G.I.F.T.

G—Generosity

Being generous is not always about handing someone money. It comes in many forms, including love. You can be sure that if you make someone feel courageous or confident, you are being generous with your words. Build people up and help them succeed. This is not the same as making it easy for them; rather, give them the encouraging words that will help them move *themselves* up. Sometimes that means giving more than you have energy for at that moment. Give when you can…and yes, that includes money, but only if and when you can afford to. Mostly, give of yourself.

I—Integrity

Be honest and do the right thing. Honesty goes a long way. Why lie? Being real with people lets you develop trust—and that helps you build a connection. Why walk over people to get what you want? You are good enough to get to where you need to be *without* knocking people down on your way. Being jealous of someone will destroy your life. Focus on where you are going and dream big for yourself. Why compare yourself to others? You are on your own journey; stay on your own course, and do not let others make you feel inferior for where you've ended up in your life. *Wherever* you are in your life, and whatever you do, be amazing at it, and give it your all.

F—Faith

Think back to when you were a child, and remember the faith that you had. It's never too late to embrace that faith again. Believe in God for everything, including a beautiful life. Life may not always be happy, so be present; find moments of beauty when, where, and how you can. Smell the aromas of life, see the colors, and taste the deliciousness of the food you eat. Faith is a state of soul; the essence of your being. You are more than the sum of your parts; you are a child of God.

T—Tenderness

Tenderness has two meanings. In the food world, it means "easy to cut or chew; not tough." In life, however, it means "showing gentleness and concern or sympathy." Sometimes you have to be tough on yourself so you are better able to be tender with others (servant leadership). In other words—to be fully human. When you are fully human, you are free to love deeply and make people feel welcome. You are more open to listening, because you are not as preoccupied with trying to fill a void or a blemish in your life. You are less likely to waste precious energy, because you are focused on living what you truly believe. God is not distant, but right by your side and all around you, just waiting for you to realize he is there for you. Embrace your faith and protect it, cherish it in others, and never settle for less. Tenderness (love of truth; truth of love) is your gauge of truth with yourself, to say nothing of others. It is both your compass and your journey's destination. It is your guide when all other sense of direction fails you. Be at one with yourself. Don't ever be afraid to be tender, especially with those you love.

Chef Table Dinners from Ennio's Notebook
Menu 4

~ Antipasti ~

Mozzarella en Carrozza

Slices of fresh mozzarella cheese dipped in a light egg batter, fried golden brown, and topped with an anchovy and parsley sauce.

~ Insalata ~

Raspberry Walnut Salad

Iceberg, romaine, and radicchio chiffonade, tossed with walnuts and raspberries, and dressed with a bright raspberry vinaigrette.

~ Entrée ~

Shrimp Veneziana

Large Gulf shrimp in a garlic/sherry sauce seasoned with basil and finished with butter. This dish is well-served over fettuccini or with rice.

Menu 4

Mozzarella en Carrozza
(appetizer; serves 4)

Ingredients:

1½ pounds	Mozzarella cheese (fresh)
4 ounces	Extra-virgin olive oil
6 ounces	Chicken stock or tomato broth
8 filets	Anchovy (chopped)
1 tablespoon	Chopped parsley
To taste	Salt and pepper
As needed	Flour (for dredging cheese)

Batter:

4 each	Eggs
1 ounce	Water
1 tablespoon	Chopped parsley
1 ounce	Grated Parmesan cheese
To taste	Salt and pepper

Preparation:

- In a bowl, combine eggs, water, chopped parsley, grated cheeses, and salt and pepper, and whisk together.
- Slice mozzarella cheese into approximately two-ounce pieces.

- Heat a large sauté pan on medium/high heat. Add two ounces of olive oil.
- While pan is heating, dredge each slice of cheese in flour and drop each one into the egg batter.
- When oil is hot, place slices of battered cheese in pan and brown on each side (more oil may be needed in cooking if it gets absorbed by the batter).
- When all cheese slices are cooked, dump off oil from hot pan, and add broth or stock to deglaze pan. Immediately add the anchovy, chopped parsley, salt and pepper, and remaining olive oil.
- Spoon on top of plated fried cheese slices.

"Mozzarella in a carriage" is typical of Southern Italian cuisine; it can be considered as "street food" too. In Campania, they sometimes sell it in street kiosks.

RASPBERRY WALNUT SALAD
(insalata; serves 4)

Ingredients:

7 ounces	Iceberg lettuce (¼" thick shred)
7 ounces	Romaine lettuce (¼" thick shred)
3 ounces	Radicchio (¼" thick shred)
2 cups	Raspberries (fresh or frozen)
1 cup	Walnut pieces
¾ cup	Extra-virgin olive oil
¼ cup	Raspberry vinegar
1 tablespoon	Brown sugar
1 teaspoon	Dijon mustard
To taste	Salt and black pepper

Preparation:

- To make the vinaigrette, place about ½ cup raspberries in a small bowl and mash them with a fork. Add raspberry vinegar and blend. Add brown sugar, Dijon mustard, olive oil, and salt and pepper. Whisk together until well blended.
- Place the romaine, iceberg, and radicchio lettuces in a large mixing bowl and toss with the raspberry vinaigrette to taste. Add in about half of the walnuts and raspberries, and toss.

- Divide salad equally between four plates, topping with re-maining raspberries and walnuts.

Radicchio is a plant that, in Italy, you can also find "in the wild." Lots of elderly people in Friuli like to go out for a walk and collect it. The wild types are often bitter. Of course, some varieties are farmed too. Radicchio comes in numerous types and colors—dark green, very dark red, etc. You can have it either in a salad or in a cooked dish. You can find radicchio in the Veneto and Friuli-Venezia-Giulia regions of northeast Italy.

SHRIMP ALLA VENEZIANA

(serves 4)

Ingredients:

24 each	Shrimp ("colossal"/ U15 size; <15 per pound)
1 tablespoon	Garlic (chopped)
4 ounces	Butter
2 ounces	Extra-virgin olive oil
3 ounces	White wine
2 ounces	Sherry wine
1 tablespoon	Pesto (or chopped fresh basil)
To taste	Salt and pepper
1½ pounds	Spinach (fresh)
1 wedge	Fresh lemon

Preparation:

- Heat a large sauté pan on medium/high heat. Add olive oil and then place shrimp in pan. When shrimp start to get a little color, flip shrimp over and add garlic to the pan (don't overcook shrimp or they will get tough).
- Add white wine to deglaze pan, then add sherry, pesto, and 3 ounces butter, along with some salt and pepper. Let simmer for a minute or two.
- Divide the shrimp equally and arrange on dinner plates, then spoon sauce on shrimp.

- Place pan back on heat, add the remaining butter, and quickly wilt the spinach, adding handfuls at a time. Add salt and pepper, and when ready, place next to plated shrimp.
- Garnish with a lemon wedge; feel free to squeeze over shrimp for added pop.

We recommend serving shrimp over fettuccine pasta, or alongside rice.

CHAPTER 5

— ❧ —

America: Part II, 1976–1984

ENNIO'S RISTORANTE (WEST ORANGE, NEW JERSEY, 1976–1980)

THE OWNER OF the Skyline, Mr. Gordon, told me in 1976 that they found a restaurant in New Jersey. If I contributed $25,000, I would be able to open the restaurant with him. We became partners. Ennio's Ristorante opened in 1976 in East Orange, New Jersey; eventually, however, I learned that Mr. Gordon was taking money from the register and I was having a hard time paying the bills. I eventually went to court against Mr. Gordon, and the judge ruled in my favor. I became the sole owner of the restaurant, and Mr. Gordon was forced out of the business. A police officer named "Moose" from East Orange used to come and eat at the restaurant a lot. He became almost like an informal bodyguard for me and made sure there was no trouble.

Ennio's Ristorante was like a regular hotel, almost like a Ramada Inn. It had a restaurant and offered breakfast, catering, and a bar. We would host showers, small weddings, and a lot of meetings. Dinner was in the dining room, and breakfast was served on the other side of the hotel, almost like a diner setting. I owned the restaurant, the bar, and the coffee shop (all of which were on the first floor), but not the hotel. We had bartenders, waiters, cashiers, and the office. Rose, alongside Judy and another woman, worked in the office. Rose worked there about three days a week.

One of the stories I always like to tell is about Whitney Houston. She used to live by my restaurant. She was maybe thirteen or fourteen years old and used to come by for breakfast and lunch with her aunt, Dionne Warwick. When it was raining, I would walk them to the car with an umbrella.

Just three months before I went to work with Resorts International, I had a few opportunities to sell the restaurant. In the end, however, we were robbed. The place was falling apart, but two guys said they would buy it in payments. Rose and I received the first payment, and then the men who were supposed to purchase it filed for bankruptcy. We probably made about $1,200 in the first payment. When we purchased it initially, we had borrowed money from Rose's father and Mildred in Cleveland. Luckily, we'd paid everyone back and made the money back; however, we still never recovered the restaurant's true value.

RESORTS INTERNATIONAL (CAPRICCIO, ATLANTIC CITY, NEW JERSEY, 1980–1984)

Rudy Mazzonelli once again called me and offered me a job at the Resorts International, to work in their restaurant, Capriccio, one of the most famous restaurants in Atlantic City.

Frank Sinatra

Insalata alla Francesco Sinatra

The Story

I met Frank at the Waldorf in 1969. I cooked many years for Frank, and he was truly one of the greatest men I have met in my life. He was a good friend, and I cooked for him for many years. In fact, I cooked for his sixty-eighth birthday on December 12, 1983, at Resorts International.

Ingredienti

1 pound arugula

2 blood oranges

3 ounces extra-virgin olive oil

1 ounce balsamic vinegar

2 ounces roasted pignoli (pine) nuts

2 ounces shaved Grana Padano

Salt and pepper to taste

Istruzioni

Wash and dry arugula.

Place in a salad bowl.

Add olive oil, balsamic vinegar, and salt and pepper; toss it.

Serve on four plates.

Garnish with peeled sliced oranges around the plates.

Top with pignoli (pine) nuts and shaved Grana Padano.

At Capriccio, I cooked tableside for many stars. I was hired to be the master chef for the rich and famous and their wonderful families.

One of the greatest and most generous celebrities I ever cooked for was Frank Sinatra. He rarely took a picture with anybody, but he did with me. He loved his mother more than anything in the world. Mothers to him were so important.

One day, he asked me, "Ennio, do you love your mother? Do you want money to send to your mother?" He gave me $500 to send to my mother and asked me for the receipt. He was a very generous man.

Frank Sinatra used to sing for the resort, and whenever he sang, he would come to the Capriccio and I would cook for him tableside. He had fettuccine, plus arugula salad with olive oil, vinegar, and Grana Padano cheese. Veal cutlet, about six ounces, sliced very thin, Milanese style (i.e., breaded and fried in butter), followed by my fruit flambé with ice cream. Barbara, his last wife, insisted that I sing Italian songs while I cooked for them. She would look at me and laugh, saying, "Oh, Torch, you can't sing." They nicknamed me Torch because of my fruit flambé.

One night, Nancy Sinatra, Frank's daughter, came to open the show. She was supposed to arrive before him, and Frank got upset with her for being late. I said to Frank, "I can cook for her; it only takes fifteen minutes." Just then, one of her singers said, "I don't eat this sh*t!" Frank got so upset. He looked at her and said, "You don't talk to my friend like that. Get out of here." Nancy ate my fettuccine with the arugula salad and went back to sing the opening night for her father without the other two girls, as Frank sent them away for offending me.

Nancy loved the arugula salad very much and asked me to bring a case of arugula for her to ship to California to her mother, Frank's ex-wife. The next morning, I made sure I had the case of arugula and brought it to the penthouse at Resorts International for her.

"How are you going to ship it to California?" I asked.

"I have a plane waiting," she replied. Can you imagine, paying for a private plane to take arugula to California? I couldn't understand that lifestyle.

The next night was a Friday, and the Sinatra's came for dinner. George H. W. Bush, then the vice president of the United States, along with some members of the intelligence agencies, plus movie stars, filled Capriccio. I cooked tableside for all of them. Barbara Sinatra came up to me afterward and whispered to me: "I want to throw a surprise party for Frank's birthday."

"When is it?" I asked.

"Tomorrow night."

"We can have it here," I said.

"No, it's too small. It's a party for four hundred people, and I want you to cook tableside."

"But I have a wedding tomorrow night," I said.

"The wedding will be over in time," she said. I asked her what time she wanted to have this surprise party.

"At four a.m.," she said. Presumably after his show, I thought.

"I can't cook for four hundred people by myself. It's impossible. I don't have time to hire the staff," I told her.

Barbara looked at me and smiled. "Just mention Frank Sinatra, and the president of the union will do anything."

I called the president of the union and asked for twenty captains and forty waiters. One captain is in charge of two tables and is also responsible for serving wine. The waiters work for the captain and serve the people. I also requested equipment that I needed to cook tableside. They gave me everything I needed and delivered it immediately. The butchers provided the meat I needed, the staff arrived, and suddenly it was Saturday night. Barbara had planes flying all over to bring people to the party. It was a huge surprise.

Around four a.m., when Frank walked in and the party erupted with cheers, he seemed so happy. When he saw me, he gave me a big hug. I was telling everyone at the party, "I don't know how I did this, ladies and gentlemen. I only had twenty-four hours to pull this thing together." I had forty flames, forty pans around me, and I could barely breathe anymore, after cooking tableside for so long. When the night was finally over, I passed out.

ॐ

A lot of famous people came to the resort—generous people too. The multimillionaire Leonard Tose, owner of the Philadelphia Eagles football team, would come by often. In the 1980s, he lost

Former East Orange Restaurateur Ennio Riga, now the manager of "Capriccio," Resorts International Hotel's top restaurant in Atlantic City, prepares an exotic dessert using his gourmet talents and showmanship to the delight of patrons

everything due to his gambling addiction and alcoholism, including his wife, who would later marry the president of Resorts International, I. G. "Jack" Davis. Tose would come to the restaurant all the time and bring many different personalities with him. He used a different menu every night. He was a very generous person. He would always tip me and once gave me $1,000.

I started to cook the fruit flambé tableside because I realized that people liked to be entertained. It wasn't just about the food. I became famous for it. Everyone would look for me and ask, "Chef Riga, would you cook for me?"

Comedian Alan King would come by often as well. He loved his cigar and my pasta. And if he performed at Resorts for seven days, he would dine at Capriccio for all seven days and would always have "Rigatoni a la Kinga." It was just a little plate of pasta.

❧

Mangia e bevi un buon vino! Viva la vita! (Eat [well] and drink good wine! Hooray to life!)

103

Tom Jones

Spaghetti ala Mamma Mia

When it comes to good eating, I think that Tom Jones is first-class, as well as a great wine connoisseur. This is one of the many dishes that I made for him. We became good friends and had a lot of fun. We used to joke about Peter Sellers, whose favorite joke was, "Does your dog bite? That is not my dog." I miss Tom dearly.

Ingredienti

12 ounces spaghetti, dry; cook al dente

1 pound fresh tomatoes, diced fine

2 ounces prosciutto, diced fine

2 ounces bacon, diced fine

2 ounces extra-virgin olive oil

2 ounces white wine

2 tablespoons chopped fresh basil

2 tablespoons fresh chopped parsley

1 ounce brandy

1 tablespoon chopped fine garlic

½ cup chopped fine red onions

Salt and pepper to taste, plus a pinch of crushed red pepper

2 tablespoons grated Grana Padano to taste

Istruzioni

Sauté bacon until crispy. Add onions, garlic, and olive oil. Sauté until onions are golden, and garlic starts to brown. Flambé with brandy; add white wine, tomatoes, and prosciutto. Add salt and pepper to taste, plus a pinch of crushed red pepper. Sauté for three minutes. Add hot pasta al dente. Add chopped basil and parsley. Toss with Grana Padano cheese. After placing the pasta on four plates, top it off with Grana Padano.

Tom Jones was best known for his hit recordings "It's Not Unusual" and "Delilah." I would cook for him on the beach in those beautiful tents. He became one of the most famous singers in England. He loved seafood. I used to cook tuna tartare and pasta for him. Sometimes, he and I would go out drinking together after the shows. We always had a great time.

One day, Rudy Mazzonelli, the vice president of Resorts and the man who got me the job, complained and told me that I could not sit with Jones anymore. I told Tom, who then called Rudy and asked him why I was told to not sit with him anymore. After listening to Rudy, he said, "Get me a private house, a limo, and put Ennio in the limo, and then he can sit with me again, and you won't have a problem anymore."

The next day, my boss told me I could sit with Tom Jones from now on.

When you work hard and you're nice to these stars, they are nice to you. Just because people are famous does not mean they have it easy. They make lots of sacrifices to get where they are. They have to get through life like everybody else. Everybody told me their troubles and I understood them. I was there to listen to them. That's all anybody really wants. To be really listened to.

Dom DeLuise used to come to the resort and tell jokes. He would say, "Give me half a portion and some appetizer."

I would take his order and one time I asked him, "Are you sure you only want a half-portion?"

"Do you know why I ordered a half-portion? Because later I can have the other half. And I will feel less guilty if I eat half a portion at a time." But he never ate only half of the portion—every night he had more than that. He loved to eat!

We also had John Cassavetes and Gena Rowlands come in when they were married. One time, Cassavetes said to me, "Ennio, I'm very sick. Just in case I never see you again, I appreciate your food and you caring for us." What wonderful people!

Ben Gazzara and his wife would come every time they were in town and request me as their chef as well. Cassavetes and Gazzara would say, "You cook for us, Ennio, whatever you want." I would cook for them tableside and try so hard to please them. They were truly wonderful people. Mr. Cassavetes passed away a few months later. I am so honored that I got a chance to meet him and cook for him.

Time and time again, stars would talk to me and I would listen like their therapist. I realized from listening to all of these stars that many depressed people worked in show business. So many lonely people. It baffled me a little.

Luciano
Pavarotti

Rigoletto
(makes 4 sandwiches)

Ingredienti

8 each Chicken cutlets, seasoned
with salt and pepper
(about 3 ounces each)
2 ounces extra-virgin olive oil
10 ounces roasted red peppers
(julienned)
8 slices Fontina cheese
(approx. 1 ounce each)
8 slices ripe tomato
4 tablespoons pesto
4 each Italian semolina roll

Istruzioni

Heat a large sauté pan on medium/high heat.
Add olive oil and brown chicken breast on both sides until fully cooked.
Chicken can be used warm directly from the pan or chilled for use later.
Cut rolls in half and spread one tablespoon of pesto on each roll.
Place two chicken cutlets on the bottom half of each roll, followed by
roasted red peppers, two slices of Fontina cheese, and two slices of tomato.
Top with second half of roll, cut in half, and enjoy.

A tavola non s'invecchia mai! (You never grow old at the dinner table!)

Luciano Pavarotti was singing for the casino, and for the three nights he was there, he came to Capriccio to eat. He was the greatest opera singer ever, in my opinion. His favorite food was the simplest food: spaghetti like his mother used to make, with tomato paste, onion, and oil. My mother used to make the same recipe. I would make it with a little red wine to give it extra taste. He seemed to like my recipe. Pavarotti was a very simple man when it came to food; he only liked products from Italy.

It is nice to know everybody. I knew everybody then, and I even sang for Pavarotti one day. We talked about opening a restaurant in New York together, but unfortunately, we were unable to make it happen.

Pavarotti's apartment in New York looked like a little deli. His favorite cheese, Grana Padano, would always be fully stocked. Grana Padano is also one of my favorite cheeses, as the adjective *Padano* refers to the Po Valley Plain area of northern Italy, not far from where I grew up. You can grill it and you can put it in pasta or in soup. It's good with everything.

Julio Iglesias

Scampi Flambé (appetizer)

The Story I made this appetizer tableside when Julio Iglesias came to the Capriccio while performing at Resorts in 1984. After he tried my food, he asked me to cook for his birthday, September 23, which was going to be a large party.

Ingredienti

20 U/15 (colossal) shrimp, peeled and deveined
½ cup butter
2 tablespoons chopped garlic
2 tablespoons chopped fresh parsley
1 tablespoon pesto
1 medium-size lemon
1 tablespoon Worcestershire sauce
4 tablespoons white wine
2 tablespoons brandy
Salt and pepper to taste
Flour

Istruzioni

Sauté garlic with butter until butter is golden-brown, using medium flame. Dredge shrimp in flour; shake excess. Add shrimp and sauté on both sides. Flambé with brandy and add wine and Worcestershire sauce. Add salt and pepper to taste. Reduce flame and sauté until half of the liquid disappears. Add lemon juice, pesto, and fresh parsley. Serve with hot Italian bread.

Cinque minuti per il primo! (Five minutes to the first course!)

⚘

The great Spanish singer Julio Iglesias came to Resorts. Whenever he ate at Capriccio, I would cook seafood or another dish with sausage, saffron, mussels, and chicken. My seafood was what he liked best; he didn't want anybody else cooking for him.

Rodney Dangerfield was another star who came to Resorts. When it came to Mr. Dangerfield, it was "what you see is what you get." Everything he did, he did it fast. In five minutes, he would finish a course. How he tasted the food, I don't know. He was a very strange man. He used to tell me that nobody respected him. I never knew what to say to that.

After he performed, he would come to Capriccio. He would order an appetizer, main course, and dessert at the same time. His explanation was that he didn't know which he would eat first, so he wanted everything together. I didn't know what to cook for him. I would tell the chef the night before, and we would make his meal and bring everything together. He liked fish, salad, and soup. He was always by himself. It would take him ten or fifteen minutes to finish eating, and then he would go right back to perform. Usually he would do an early and a late show. He was very nervous, especially before the shows.

⚘

I was given the opportunity to audition for a Chef Boyardee tomato sauce TV commercial.

"Should I go?" I asked Rose.

"Yes, go," she said. I went to audition for this commercial, where a lot of actors and actresses were auditioning.

They said, "Mr. Riga, it's your turn." They gave me a can of tomato sauce.

I said, "Ladies and gentleman, I'm a chef. I don't like this sauce. I don't want to use it. Give the part to someone who needs it. I don't need it. I just came because my agent told me to."

I left and went back home. When I saw Rose, I said, "Rose, I screwed up."

The next day, however, I got a call from them. They gave me the part! At that particular time, Enzo Stuarti, an Italian American tenor and musical theater performer, was there, and I had problems with him. The agency told me, "Ennio, you are a chef, and you can write the commercial." I was at this commercial, singing with the children, but Stuarti wanted to do that. I wrote the commercial, and I taught the kids to sing. He came to me and told me that he was a star and that the job should be his.

"But I wrote the commercial," I told him. I was also angry because Stuarti popularized the phrase, "That's a'Nice!" (for Ragú spaghetti sauce), and I was the one who had used it first, on set. I had a little temper tantrum, and in retaliation for this exchange, I punched him. We both lost the commercial. Later on, Stuarti and I ran into each other at Resorts. He asked me to forgive him. We gave each other a big hug and forgave each other. But losing that commercial probably cost me about half a million dollars.

I also made a program called "Kids Can Cook Too," but this was on later, after the Stuarti incident. In the program, I taught children how to cook. I did it twice.

When I was offered the second commercial job, I once again said, "Give it to somebody who needs it." But they wanted a chef with a famous name. I made about $1,300 every couple of months that it was aired. It was a national campaign, and it was first aired in California. I had to do about one hundred takes because I have a heavy accent and couldn't pronounce the word *fork* clearly. Everybody was cracking up, but the company that paid for the commercial was irked because they were paying $5,000 an hour to tape the commercial. It took me a whole day to tape it.

After it aired, the next time I ran into Frank Sinatra, he said, "Torch! You're more famous than me! I saw you on television." In life, you make a lot of friends, but to me, Frank Sinatra was a special one. He asked me if I wanted to go to California and open up a restaurant. He also said that if anybody bothered me, I should let him know.

In 1980, I met Tony Orlando. He was singing in an opening act at Resorts. He was there with his father, and I cooked tableside for them.

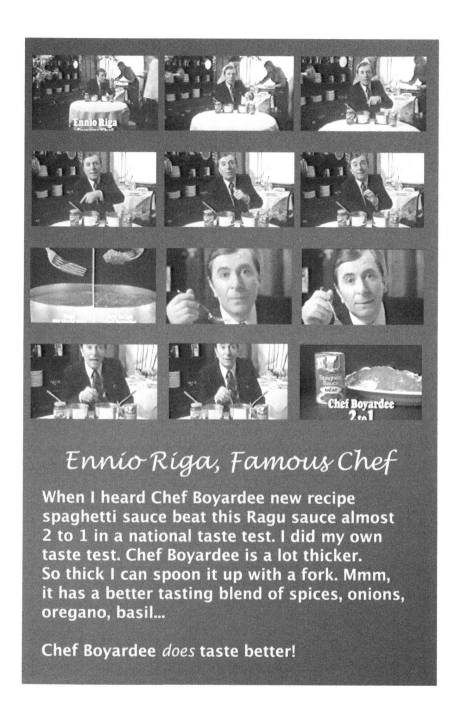

Ennio Riga, Famous Chef

When I heard Chef Boyardee new recipe spaghetti sauce beat this Ragu sauce almost 2 to 1 in a national taste test. I did my own taste test. Chef Boyardee is a lot thicker. So thick I can spoon it up with a fork. Mmm, it has a better tasting blend of spices, onions, oregano, basil...

Chef Boyardee *does* taste better!

His father was crazy about my seafood. He also liked a rack of lamb, which I would cook tableside. I would slice the racked lamb tableside; make a lamb sauce, and sauté spinach with butter and garlic. I would then put the spinach on the bottom of the plate, lamb on top, and finish off the meal with a fruit flambé.

After Tony and his father finished, we sat down together and talked about his problems. Tony was really down. I said to him, let me talk with some people who might be able to help you. I had connections. I helped him get jobs. He wanted to open a restaurant. They called it the Italian Greek Forum. It consisted of a blend of Italian and Greek foods.

The last night I cooked at Resorts was for Frank Sinatra. One of the patrons came in with his wife. He wasn't wearing a jacket. The dress code at Capriccio was very specific and strict: everyone must wear a jacket.

This man was a Mafia hit man. I did not know this at the time. I also did not know that he had just come from the casino after losing $50,000. When this man came in for dinner, I reminded him of the dress code, which he scoffed at. I went and found him a spare red jacket that we had in the back and asked him to wear it. It made him look a little ridiculous, I guess, though that was not my intent.

"I don't want to wear this," he said angrily.

"I will not serve you unless you wear a jacket," I said firmly. He put the jacket on and looked me right in the face.

"Ennio, you're a dead man."

I ignored the comment and proceeded to cook for him. As I cooked tableside, I realized who he was, the connections he had, and what his reputation was. I finished the meal. Later that evening, the pit boss from the casino called Capriccio looking for me. The pit boss was also affiliated with the Mafia.

"Ennio, go home and don't come back until I call you," he said. I left, and Rose and I wondered what would happen. We knew and had seen how the Mafia ran everything.

Two days later, the pit boss called and said, "I straightened everything out; it's okay for you to come back." I went back to work, and Rose joined me for dinner. At one point, the pit boss entered Capriccio and approached Rose and me.

"Everything's okay," he repeated. "You don't have to worry. I straightened it out. But now you owe me."

As he walked away, we were a little startled and silent for a moment. Then Rose said, "That's it, Ennio. We're leaving and never coming back." We did not want to owe a Mafia man. I didn't want to be involved in that type of environment anymore. I did not want to put my family at risk because someone was inappropriately dressed at my restaurant.

I left Resorts for good.

Julie's Reflections

Over the following years, Dad went work in Atlantic City. He came home on Monday, left to go back Thursday morning, and was gone for most of the weekend. Every time my father took a photo with a celebrity, my mother would bring it to the Union Flea Market to get it framed in gold. She worked hard to create the "wall of fame" in our basement, which became the centerpiece of all our parties. Later on, we recreated this wall of fame at Riga's Trottoria, and then again, in the Florida house.

Mom kept us busy at the mall and took us to lunch, and she would also take us to Atlantic City quite often. We went to all the shows, were privileged enough to eat at the Capriccio, and were comped all over. Mom and Dad had a little apartment in Margate, which was within walking distance from Capriccio. Mom told me that we would eat breakfast there and then go out for the day.

When I ask my mom and sister about all that we did in Atlantic City now, however, I get two different stories. I apparently have few to no memories, and I wish I could call Dad and ask him, because he would know the truth. It is so funny how we all have a different story.

Ennio's Wall of Fame

Joan Rivers

Andy Gibb

Frankie Valli

Art Carney

Ennio's Wall of Fame

Tom Jones

Tony Bennett

Sheena Easton

Julio Iglesias

Debbie Reynolds

Rose Riga

It sounds like we went to Atlantic City a lot on the weekends. My sister was six and I was eight. I went to see Tony Orlando and sat right up front. After the show, we went backstage and he gave me an album. This was probably the first record I owned. I listened to "Knock Three Times" and "Tie a Yellow Ribbon" like it was going out of style. Mom said that we would go to see a show and then have dinner at Capriccio. She said we went to shows and met people like Wayne Newton, Frank Sinatra, and Bobby Vinton, and we even had lunch with Tom Jones. Debbie said that we briefly met Frank Sinatra and saw him sing from the hallway, because for some reason, they did not let us into the show that night. We spent a lot of time in the hotel, and Debbie said that the photographer from the restaurant, who later became a famous model, watched us.

We ate at AC's best restaurants. I learned early on that I loved shrimp and good food. Going to AC was the only real time we would spend with my dad, because he was so busy with this job. I do remember Dad leaving in a limo the day he did the Chef Boyardee TV commercial, and I was so embarrassed when he did the fruit flambé on "Live with Regis and Kathy Lee." My dad had an incredible career, and it seemed like he was truly rocking it in Atlantic City. As you may know, the AC crowd was "interesting," and when things got a little scary, he left for a more stable job that was only twenty minutes from home. We sort of had our dad back…but not really, because he was still always working. Dad loved working for Prime Hospitality with David Simon. He really loved him, and together they became very successful.

He was the corporate chef, with tons of responsibility for people, food cost, and creating recipes. Dad loved to work. It was who he was. He was a model of someone who loved his job. He always told me that if you love your job, you never work a day in your life. I guess my father was not working, since he truly loved what he did, and he loved being able to provide for us.

Helen Hollander's Reflections
(Helen is Rose Riga's younger sister.)

I had the privilege of knowing Ennio for forty-four years. When my sister married him, I suddenly had not only a brother-in-law but another roommate. We all lived in a small house in Union, New Jersey. We all managed to get along, and now we had a personal chef and an extra set of hands to help my father around the house. Ennio was happy to do whatever he could. He and my father got along great, and my parents welcomed this Italian man into our Jewish household. Ennio introduced our family to the flavors of Italy, including tripe—we were schooled fast on Italian cooking!

As time went on, they moved out and started some new Riga traditions, like the Riga Christmas party and the annual summer picnic. Anyone who knew the Riga's was invited to both. It was like attending a bar mitzvah or a wedding. Ennio served buffet-style with every food you can imagine. We always had a great time.

Ennio had a passion for life and success, an inner confidence that allowed him to try anything. He loved America and was proud to be an American. He enjoyed not only cooking, but also fishing, soccer, and gardening, fueled by a true passion for his family and life. He truly lived a fascinating life and strived to make his children's lives better than his own.

David Solomon's Reflections

A lot of the stories are fuzzy (because every time we got together, we had enough to make everything fuzzy)...but I remember the very first time I met him, at a family event in Hillside (Union). Ennio and Rose lived upstairs; I think Julie was already born....I had just met Gail, we were going together, and she invited me to this family get-together. When I walked in, everybody just kind of stared...except for Ennio! He said, "Hey, you! Come sit down next to me." He had one of these big gallon jugs of wine and started pouring drinks...and after a while, the whole experience didn't look so scary to me...and he said to me, "I like you, and you're going to be in this family." We became family, even though we always said we were the outlaws!

☙

Leadership Lesson 5: Authentic Grieving

The day my father died, I cried and cried. The patriarch of our family was no longer here to talk to for guidance, love, and support; it was such a huge loss for all of us. Thankfully, my father knew he was going to leave us and had prepared us all for this day. I am not going to say I was ready for him to go, but I was more ready than the others. He told me, time and time again, "Although I will not be with you physically, somehow, I will remain with you and never leave you." He also left me his life story, along with a host of life lessons. We also believe that my father went to heaven and that we will all be reunited one day—a comfort to the soul.

At the beginning of this book, I shared my story about crying in Trader Joe's, and how it taught me acceptance about grieving my own way. How did I do this?

- Finished my dad's life story—such a healing activity. Just documenting a life, and ferreting out the stories of your childhood, is extremely therapeutic.
- Collected all of my dad's shirts and made a quilt out of them.
- Made a photo collage of my dad and hung it up for a long, long time.
- Initiated traditions: every Father's Day, I make sauce and sing Italian songs.

- Have a good cry every time a song comes on that reminds me of my dad.
- Remember him most days, even without prompting!

In whatever ways grieve—grieve authentically (and unapologetically)!

Chef Table Dinners from
Ennio's Notebook
Menu 5

~ Antipasti ~

Filetto di Pollo Freddo

Fresh chicken tenders marinated in lemon, Dijon mustard, honey, and extra-virgin olive oil, coated with sesame seeds and baked. Finished with chopped cilantro and served with a ranch dressing.

~ Insalata ~

Insalate Della Casa

Torn romaine leaves with black olives, diced ripe tomatoes, cucumber juliennes, and red onion, tossed in a garlic balsamic vinaigrette and finished with croutons and shaved Asiago cheese.

~ Entrée ~

Spaghettini Puttanesca

Fresh ripe tomatoes, garlic, olives, capers, and anchovies, simmered in a bit of chicken stock and white wine, seasoned with fresh basil and a pinch of oregano. Served over al dente spaghettini with a generous helping of grated Parmesan cheese and a twist of the pepper mill.

Menu 5

Filetto di Pollo Freddo
(appetizer; serves four)

Ingredients:

20 each	Chicken tenders
1.5 ounces	Lemon juice
2 ounces	Honey
1 ounce	Dijon mustard
1 ounce	Sesame seeds
2 ounces	Extra-virgin olive oil (garlic flavored preferred)
1 tablespoon	Cilantro (chopped)
1 each	Lemon (cut in quarters for garnish)

Preparation:

- Place lemon juice, honey, and Dijon mustard in a bowl and mix together.
- Add the chicken tenders and mix so all the chicken tenders are coated with the mixture. Cover and marinate in refrigerator overnight.
- When ready for service, preheat oven to 450°.
- Coat a sheet pan with the olive oil.
- Add sesame seeds to chicken tenders and mix so the seeds are evenly dispersed.

- Lay out each chicken tender onto the sheet pan, and place in the oven.
- Bake until cooked and crispy.
- Plate five chicken tenders on each plate, and sprinkle with cilantro; serve with a lemon wedge.
- Serve with ranch dressing (or any favorite dressing).

Also delicious cold!

INSALATE DELLA CASA
(insalata; serves four)

Ingredients:

16 ounces	Romaine lettuce (torn into 2-inch pieces)
2 tablespoons	Black olives (sliced)
2 each	Red onion (sliced ¼ inch thick)
8 ounces	Ripe tomato (diced)
8 each	Cucumber slices (julienne)
2 cups	Croutons
4 tablespoons	Asiago cheese (shaved)
¾ cup	Extra-virgin olive oil
¼ cup	Balsamic vinegar
1 teaspoon	Fresh garlic, chopped
To taste	Salt and black pepper

Preparation:

- To make the vinaigrette, in a small bowl, place olive oil, balsamic vinegar, garlic, and salt and pepper. Whisk together until well blended.
- Place the romaine lettuce in a large mixing bowl, and toss with balsamic vinaigrette to taste.
- Add black olives, diced tomato, and cucumber juliennes and toss.

- Just before serving, add croutons and toss.
- Divide salad equally among four plates, top with red on-ion rings and shaved Asiago cheese, and serve.

SPAGHETTINI ALLA PUTTANESCA

(serves four)

Ingredients:

1 pound	Spaghettini (uncooked); this is a thinner version of spaghetti
2 tablespoons	Garlic (chopped)
3 ounces	Extra-virgin olive oil
2 ounces	Chicken stock
2 ounces	White wine
14 ounces	Chopped plum tomatoes
1 tablespoon	Fresh basil (chopped)
16 each	Black olives (whole)
2 tablespoons	Capers
8 filets	Anchovies (chopped fine)
1 pinch	Oregano
1 ounces	Butter
1 cup	Grated Parmesan cheese
To taste	Black pepper

Preparation:

- Put on a pot of salted boiling water to cook pasta.
- Heat a large sauté pan on medium/high heat. Add olive oil and lightly sauté garlic in pan. Add chopped plum tomatoes, bring to a simmer, and cook for about five minutes. Add white wine, chicken stock, anchovies, capers, black

olives, basil, oregano, and black pepper. Bring to a simmer and cook for another few minutes, then add butter to finish the sauce.

- While the mixture simmers, cook pasta to al dente, strain, and then add the hot pasta to puttanesca sauce in pan and toss. Reserve some pasta water to moisten the pasta, if necessary.
- Plate equally; garnish with fresh basil leaves; top with grated Parmesan cheese.

CHAPTER 6

America: Part III, Still in My Prime, 1984 – 2003

THE DAY AFTER Rose and I decided it was time for me to leave Resorts, I went to interview at Prime Hospitality, which is a chain of hotels and restaurants. Peter E. Simon, who I met at Resorts and is the father of David Simon, is the one who helped me get the job. I went in for an interview, and a half-hour later, I had a new job. I gave notice to my boss at Resorts, and a week later I was officially working with Prime Hospitality.

One of the assignments from corporate was to bring the food cost down from 37 percent to 32 percent. In my first meeting, I grabbed a garbage bag in front of all of these big shots dressed in nice suits. I didn't drop the garbage bag (which contained all of the wasted food) on the floor. Instead, I dropped it right on the table in front of them. When it came to food, they did not know how to save money…so I began to teach them how to use the wasted food. I showed them how to make soups and meatballs from the leftovers; there was no reason to be wasting as much as they were. Leftovers could be made into new delicious meals while still fresh, and they were great for buffets at the bar. I changed all of the menus, ordering procedures, and more—and then I went on vacation.

After I'd been working at Prime Hospitality for a while, I met Peter E. Simon again, and he said to me, "I can't believe what you did! I have been trying for twenty years to bring the food cost down, and you did it in a month. I asked you to bring food cost down to 32 percent, and you brought it down to 29 percent." They had apparently paid a million dollars for a consulting company to come in to bring the food cost down, with no improvements. The big shots wanted to know how I did it.

"You paid a company one million dollars, and you want *me* to tell you how to do it? You need to pay me." I became the food-cost guru. People started to get jealous of me. In the end, however, I succeeded in what I did—a true expert. I never let any of their negativity bother me.

I stayed at Prime Hospitality for twenty years and accomplished plenty. Mr. Simon once said, "When I bought the Ramada chain, I made $1 million. When I hired Ennio, I made $10 million." That meant a lot to me, because it showed how hard I worked, as well as how essential I was to the business.

In 1984, the first year I was there, Regis Philbin called and wanted me to do a show again. I went to New York and did a second show. What a nice guy! We did the show together, and it was a great success with the flambé—a remarkable and rewarding moment. I missed my celebrity days, but had a greater purpose in my new job: to mentor and help others succeed as well.

In this job, I had ups and downs. You have to remember, when you work for a big chain restaurant, you work with good and bad people. You have to learn to deal with any circumstance. Sometimes you get a boss with whom you just don't agree. This applies to any type of job. My boss at that particular time liked to use packaged food; I was against it. I only wanted to use fresh products in my restaurant.

In fact, one of those food demonstrations may have been one of the funniest frenzies we have ever seen. It was performed by Ennio Riga, the maître d' of Resorts' Capriccio Restaurante, and fruit salad will never be the same again. Accompanied by a guitarist, Ennio peeled oranges, apples and pineapples while singing Italian love songs. His piece de resistance, however, was his dissection of a banana while he samba'd to La Cumbachero.

"A-cumba-cumba-cumba-cumbachero!" Mind-boggling.

One time, he came up to me with a plastic bag and a pair of scissors—packaged food for the beef stew we were supposed to be offering that night.

"Do you want to try *my* beef stew?" I asked.

"No, I use my own products," he said, and he walked away, leaving me with the plastic bag and scissors. I was disgusted that we were not using fresh food to create dishes for our customers.

For twenty years, I had to deal with people like him. They screwed the company for those twenty years, and I felt like I was the only one trying to *save* the company. One time, another genius wanted to do a promotion, so he purchased ten thousand steaks. He wanted to have the hotels push it as a special, where we'd sell the steaks for $9.99. At the end of the day, they lost $3,000. I told the boss, "Don't do it; they don't know what they're doing." They did not listen to me.

Every year I worked for Prime, things became tougher and tougher. In 1981, I went to Armonk, New York, to check reservations for a party of about two hundred the following night. I noticed lots of leaves and garbage piled up, and I told them we couldn't leave the garbage there. One of the employees complained about me. In the end, he was fired, and they agreed with me. Simple as that.

In 1987, the electricity went out as I was hosting a private dinner party for three hundred people. All of the stoves shut down. How am I going to make dinner now for three hundred people… with baked potatoes? I used three conventional ovens, and in the stove was the baked potato, and I put the prime ribs on top. Nobody would ever believe that I made dinner in time—without electricity or gas. Each table had beautiful candles. Another one of my miracles.

One year, three days before Christmas, we had hundreds of people who made reservations for the first lunch seating, and another few hundred people for the second lunch seating. For dinner, same story. I did it without sweating. I had to make eighteen different sauces. Everybody was nervous...but that turned out to be a big money day for Prime Hospitality.

Another time, they had a fundraiser for President George H. W. Bush. I never had any problems, because I had taken care of presidents before and the FBI knew me. Somehow, though, my staff disappeared. We had five hundred people for the buffet. It went smoothly. People were able to take a picture with the president. I even took a picture with the president and his mother. He was very nice. I voted for him.

Prime Hospitality had a hotel in Vegas, and in 1994 I was out there doing a banquet for them. Just as I was preparing to get my fruit flambé ready, I received a phone call from my wife. My mother had died. I called my boss, and she told me that I had to go. I left for Italy. The next morning, I made it just before they closed the coffin.

In September the following year, I was in charge of four hundred general managers all over the country. They asked me once again to go to Vegas and make them dinner. Everybody was waiting for my fruit flambé act. And guess what? I received a phone call from David Simon that my father had passed away.

"Your father died; you have to go," he said.

"No, I have to do the show," I replied. It was the toughest thing. Tears were streaming down my cheeks. And at the end, I pointed to the sky and said, "This is for you, Papa." I looked at the people, and they had tears in their eyes. They said it was the best show I ever did. Afterward, I went home from Las Vegas to New Jersey, got my passport, packed, and headed to the airport. When I got there, I was so tired. I made it just in time, once again, to say goodbye to my papa.

After the funeral, I asked my sister for a cup of chamomile tea. I wasn't feeling well. I was exhausted. We got into an argument and began to fight. I traveled to my nephew's home and never went back to my childhood home again. After my parents died, I went back to Italy several times for vacation, but I would stay with either my nephew or my brother, Galdino. I would not speak to my sister.

Not long after my father died, I became ill with a 105-degree fever. I went to the hospital and passed out. I felt like I was dreaming. I saw this beautiful light. In front of me was Jesus. When you look into Jesus's eyes, you see eternity. You must go through Him to get into heaven, but every time I walked through Him, He was standing in front of me again. I couldn't get into heaven. I was in the limbo between, facing Jesus. I can't describe the light to you in simple words. It was like the moon, the stars, something amazing. Through the light, I suddenly saw my mother. She was sitting in a rocking chair knitting.

"What are you doing here? It isn't your time yet," she told me.

"Your **mission** is not over yet; you need to go back," Jesus said.

"I want to stay here...I have no pain," I said to them. But came back. I woke up and was in so much pain. They put me in a tub full of ice. I was in the hospital for about a week or two. have no idea what happened to me. They tried to find out wha was wrong with me at the hospital, but nothing was wrong. I do truly believe I saw heaven. When I went to heaven, it was beautiful—but I had to come back to finish my **mission** and stay on my course.

Luckily, I got better, and life continued. The headquarters of Prime Hospitality was on Route 46 in Fairfield, New Jersey. They had a restaurant there but it never did much business. David Simon suggested putting an Italian name on it, because he believed that would build up the business and customer flow. They tried several names, but none worked. I said, "If you add a personal touch, it might help." They decided to open a pizzeria-type place like they do in Italy, and we called it Riga. With all the cheeses, beautiful antipasti, and Italian delicacies, we started to build and build. We worked so hard, really day and night. I have many great memories and what an amazing staff I had!

One day, David Simon said to me, "You never had three hundred people in the restaurant."

I said, "I'll show you. I will have three hundred people this weekend."

I won the bet. He still hasn't paid me.

Inside Riga, David wanted pictures of me with movie stars and celebrities framed and placed around the lobby. We bought new plates, new dishes. We went on television; we were written about in the newspaper. Life was good.

The Riga experience is modeled after a Northern Italian trattoria. At the heart of the trattoria concept are Riga's unsurpassed pizza and foccacia cooked in an authentic wood-burning oven, with splendid aromas permeating the entire room. The irresistible menu features grilled specialties and abundant classic selections, masterfully prepared with old country flair, and embellished by a host of salads, fresh pastas, breads and marvelous desserts. Riga is designed to host groups for special functions, and provides an uniquely rewarding Sunday Brunch.

Because of my knowledge and hard work, I was one of the corporate managers for thirteen hundred Prime Hospitality hotels. After so many years with Prime, Sheraton Hotels and restaurants came in. They never did exceptionally well. I suggested to them, "Why don't we open a restaurant with the name Riga?" Riga, an Italian Trattoria. And they said, "Sure!"

I had a pizza oven. The pizza was so good…and then I had a very nice restaurant. From Milano, I had risotto alla Milanese. From Geneva, I had puttanesca, which started in World War II. They didn't have time to eat, so they created this quick dish. I wanted to implement that into my restaurant. After we made renovations and changed the restaurant name to Riga, they made huge profits off the opening banquet. We had so many people there…and all the greatest food in the world. It was beautiful! We had such a good time. After the banquet, I got so busy.

My reputation spoke for itself, and my restaurant was doing very well. I didn't have to advertise anymore. Each day by two p.m., my restaurant was completely full.

One day, I went behind the bar to fix some drinks for the waiters and saw a brown box under the table. Written on the box was, "I hope you die." I called the police right away. Two police officers showed up and told me we had to evacuate the restaurant.

"I have hundreds of people here; I can't evacuate," I said.

"Sir, we are going to have to call the fire department and the FBI."

"Could we take away the box?"

"No way," the officer said.

"I'm going to take the box out of the building," I said. They clearly thought I was crazy. Here was the parking lot of my restaurant, filled with policemen and arriving firefighters, and I lift the box and start to walk away very gently. When the FBI showed up, they asked me why I did that. I said I could not let anyone in my restaurant get hurt; a lot of children were present, and I couldn't take that chance. I took the box and walked across the street with it.

The FBI told me it was the stupidest thing to do, but they congratulated me for my courage. The dogs came barking. They opened up the box, and it was a clock. Later, we found out my bartender did it. They arrested him and the other man in on it with him.

℘

After 9/11, everything changed and a lot of people lost their businesses. I had to work harder. I was sixty-three and getting near retirement. Another company, the Blackstone Group, eventually bought the company, on August 18, 2004. Once I retired, Riga went under. After all, what is Riga without Riga? They lost everything. It went down to zero. They just kept it open for hotel clients to have breakfast. They had no idea how to run a restaurant or how to bring food cost down. Why didn't they let a professional do the job? They lost the chef…and then they lost my customers.

When I had first come to Prime Hospitality, Peter E. Simon was running the business. He was a nice man. He was the father of David, who became my boss. Both are great men. Others within Prime Hospitality tried to ban me from talking to them. I said it was a free country. I felt that certain people put pressure on me in every way possible to make me quit. They put me in the kitchen because they fired my shift. I would work twenty-hour shifts and break my back doing so. One day, I got sick and went to the hospital from working so much. Why do people have to be so stupid? Because they are jealous and don't know what they are doing, yet they want to get credit (e.g., for cutting food cost).

When it comes to food costs…and perhaps life overall…you must have integrity, and you must watch your waste. One waste type goes in the garbage; the others can be reused. So many people waste so much food. People all over the world are dying of hunger, and people here in America waste 35 percent of their food by throwing it in the garbage. For twenty-seven years, I fought to change that. I wanted to preserve as much food as we could.

One time, this man came in with the milk delivery and stole lobster right out of the freezer. I followed him to the parking lot and took pictures of him. I called the police. Watch your back, watch the front door, and watch the back door, and you will be successful. Train the waiters to be careful.

Perhaps you have heard of the Venezuelan mystic Maria Esperanza Medrano de Bianchini. In her book, she wrote that two planes would come from the sky and bring destruction. One day, I was talking to this lady on the phone and she said, "I'm there with you." It was Maria Esperanza! She told me she would see me soon.

That following Saturday night, I needed a table for eighteen people, but the restaurant was booked. I didn't know how I was going to accommodate all of these people. Suddenly, all of my clients who had reservations called to cancel, all for different reasons. Maria Esperanza told me that I would have the table I needed in fifteen minutes...and it happened! It was a miracle. Maria Esperanza arrived, along with her sons and Father Meduno, and I finally met this wonderful lady. She liked me. I had my family there and a few friends. Maria Esperanza didn't order anything—just water.

"What do you want to eat?" I asked her.

"She doesn't eat anything when she goes out, because she is afraid of being contaminated with the Devil," one of her sons said. I looked at her.

"Do you trust me?"

"Yes, I do," she replied. I cooked fettuccine for her and she ate it all. Everybody looked at me. They couldn't believe it! She never ate food from anybody.

I brought my chefs out that night to meet this amazing person. She then told one of my staff that he had had an accident when he was young and then a seizure. How did she know this? Maria Esperanza was a really exceptional woman. She asked me to take a picture with her. At one point, she got up and walked away from us, and Father Meduno leaned in to ask me something.

"Do you think she likes me?" he asked.

"I don't know if she likes you. I just met you today." That was my response to him. I did not feel that I could speak for her. I was talking to her that night, and I could see the light. She looked like a saint to me. She visited the restaurant a couple more times after that.

One man I knew had terminal cancer, and he wanted to follow her. He was going to die. I took him to see her. Maria Esperanza took him to the hospital, and minutes later, they said he was free of cancer. They asked her how she did that.

"I didn't do that. I just asked Jesus to save his life, and he did," she replied. This man had cancer all over his body. Now I truly believed this woman is a saint.

She said to me one time, "Ennio, you are so special. You don't even know." She had the two stigmata of Jesus coming out of her hands and roses coming out of her heart. She smelled like roses. She told me a story of how Mother Teresa fell extremely ill at one point. Maria Esperanza asked God not to take her, and Mother Teresa got better right away.

Mother Teresa performed a lot of miracles that people didn't know about...and Maria Esperanza, Mother Teresa, Pope John Paul II, and Padre Pio were all connected to each other. I have a rosary that was sent to me by Pope John Paul II through Mother

Teresa. Both the Pope and Maria Esperanza had Parkinson's disease.

The last time I saw Maria Esperanza, she said to me, "I'll see you on the other side." I didn't understand that, but I know this: love and the divine transcend this world, and it was as if she did too. She was a very special person. When I was around her, I felt like I was already in heaven.

I remember the day I decided I wanted to write this book, and I asked my nurse to help me with it. I went to look in my closet for some magazines, and boom…Maria Esperanza's book fell on my feet. I had never read her book before. And then something else fell on my foot: the picture of Maria Esperanza with me. It had to be a sign.

When I went to heaven and saw my mother and Jesus, they told me it wasn't my time yet. I didn't understand. Maybe my mission is to finish this book.

I hope that after reading this, you feel like you know me. By now, you must realize I have met a lot of people—celebrities, kings and queens, religious figures, and regular people—but in God's eyes, we are all equal.

❦

Julie's Reflections

Growing up, my father always made enough money to provide for our family. Mom stayed home, and we did not want for anything. He paid my college tuition and board, and covered all of my financial needs. While I was in college, Dad often told the story about when he dropped me off at college for the first time. He was so proud but so scared that I was not going to really want to stay there. I ran after the car waving as they left, and then I went inside and started making friends. My parents really encouraged me to stay in college, and it was truly one of the greatest experiences of my life. Later on, after I completed my graduate degree, Dad was so proud of me. He hung a copy of my graduate school diploma in his office.

When Dad opened Riga's, I was in my early twenties, and it was so much fun to have a restaurant named after my dad—and me! Riga and Italian trattoria were quite popular in the area. Dad was very busy and had some very special customers. Riga's restaurant drew quite a diverse crowd, from the New Jersey Devils to Maria Esperanza. Dad became great friends with New Jersey Devils head coaches Jacques Lemaire and Larry Robinson. All of the players spent many nights at the hotel during the years they won the Stanley Cup. We even have a jersey and a watch to prove it.

Early on, I had the chance to work at Riga. It was interesting to work for my dad. Running a restaurant is stressful, because your goal is to make people happy by providing delicious hot food on time. My father wanted everyone's experience to be just that. He spent so much time forging relationships with people so that they would feel welcome. If a food item was not to your liking, you could send it back until it came out right (and not have to worry about my dad punching you). People appreciated his attention to detail and his warm, welcoming demeanor. I learned so much from him.

In my later twenties, I had the opportunity to spend my Saturday nights dining at the restaurant. It was then that I started to get to know my dad in a new way. I was able to look to him more as a mentor and coach, and I truly wanted to hear what he had to say.

In my early twenties, I started going to church and learning more about God. My sister started going to temple to do the same. It was a crazy time for my parents. Suddenly, they had two children searching for spirituality. My sister went to Israel briefly and ended up having an arranged marriage. I ended up meeting a man at church. Interestingly, both of those marriages ended up short-lived. Even so, my dad provided us both with weddings. This was what he had been waiting for. He always dreamed of dancing with us at our weddings, and because of crazy religious rules, he did not get to do so with either of us. I know that sounds terrible—and it really was. I am still upset that we did not get to honor his wishes.

My sister became a Lubavitch (Chabad) Jew, which is related to Hasidic Jews. These people keep kosher, wear wigs and skirts, and try to follow a slew of rules. They have to call rabbis to see if they can do certain things or eat certain foods. This was hard on all of us. My sister was no longer able to really eat with us, and Dad had a hard time cooking for her. Picture my Italian father sitting with all of these bearded men. He attended a lot of parties where he was the only non-bearded man and sat with them while they sang, drank, and prayed. It was a sight to see, and Dad had many funny things to say about this experience.

My sister was married in Crown Heights, New York, and had a religious wedding. Dad could not even walk her up to the rabbi, because he was not Jewish. He was sad about this, but nevertheless he still paid for the wedding. He could not take part in any of the cooking, but he did get to buy the alcohol.

My wedding was at his hotel, the Radisson. He was in charge of everything. He cooked and prepared a lot of the food that day. I did not get to go to my cocktail hour, but I was told that it was so amazing that people still talk about it. He did a flambé and had the most amazing dessert room. This was the wedding of all weddings for him, and he did everything he could to make it such a great day. I kind of wish I could go back to that day, just to see everything he did to make it amazing, from the ice sculptures to the showmanship in everything he did. This was his chance (and really, his only chance) to do his own daughter's wedding. Dad worked with so many brides and families to help them make their days great during his career, but this was his chance to do his own daughter's. While this was a great accomplishment for him, he worked so hard that I am not sure how much he really enjoyed it. Dad always worked hard, because he wanted to excel in everything he did. In his heart, he loved making people happy.

Whenever he served people, he often ended it with, "It was all my pleasure." He truly maintained a mantra of service.

David Simon's Reflections

Ennio and I had a very special relationship. My fondest memory was for several years in the early to late 1990s, I would come into work on Saturday mornings around seven-thirty a.m. Usually within the hour, Ennio would come up from the restaurant to my office, and with that knowing smile, he would tell me how many covers they did at Riga's on Friday night and guesstimate how many they would do on Saturday. I'd usually try and make a dollar bet with him. No matter what number he said he would do on Saturday, I would tell him, "No way, you'll never do that." We'd bet the buck, and of course I was always rooting for him to be correct. He won about 90 percent of the time, and we were both ecstatic to see the business thrive.

Those Saturdays also gave Ennio time to gripe about anything that was on his mind. Usually it was about the laziness of the next generation. "They just don't have the love," he would tell me. No one was more loyal or dedicated to his job and his company than Ennio. Even at his most frustrated, he would say, "I love this company"…and he did!

Ennio taught me what it meant to be a fighter. When I got sick, he kept telling me everything was going to be okay, but "You have to fight, David," he would say constantly.

He fought his whole life for everything he achieved—no easy thing. I loved his stories of how he fed the Jewish family when the Nazis were out looking for them…of him and Franco on the QE II, and how he saved Franco's a** one night when some guys were looking to beat him up. I marveled at his stories of serving Mr. Frank Sinatra at the Waldorf…but most of all, I liked his story of his cousin Battista. I'm not really sure if Battista truly existed, but to listen to Ennio discuss Battista's manhood size was something of a legend. Every time he heard the name Battista, he would laugh with that special Ennio laugh that I wish I could hear now.

I didn't realize Ennio liked to play the slot machines and black-jack until after he retired. I'd meet him at one of the many Florida casinos, and we'd be partners in whatever we'd play. One day I think I won $1,000 at the blackjack table and gave half of it to Ennio. I then left, thinking he would be leaving as well, only to find out that he stayed…and probably walked into his house with a mere fifty dollars. He really enjoyed the slots.

It's amazing that he and I would be such close friends, as we came from completely different backgrounds and experiences… but we grew to love and respect each other unconditionally. He treated me and my family like royalty, and my children were his biggest fans. When we'd go out as a family and eat at Riga's, it was a feast like no other. He'd always make my favorite dish, Farfalle ala David (on the menu and named after me). It was just pasta with chicken, garlic, and olive oil, but it was delicious every time. And who could forget his poached pears, not to mention (in his earlier days) the flambé show! I thought he would die of a heart attack doing that, but it was his signature item, and he absolutely loved performing it.

Mostly I remember his compassion for the people who meant something to him—his family, of course, but also guys he worked with: Peter Marino, Franco, Lou Lamoriello, Tim Lauch, Rosalie Buttros, the accountant, and many more.

In a word, Ennio was *caring*. He cared for everyone who came into his world: the guests who dined at Riga's, the servers who waited on the guests, his bosses, his colleagues, and his family. Ennio never forgot where he came from, and he considered himself the luckiest guy in the world. While he didn't have all the riches, he had love and respect from all who really knew him—and that's all he really cared about.

Bob Garvey's Reflections

I had the special privilege of working with Ennio at Prime Hospitality, where I helped him open up hotel restaurants and comply with food cost and service. Although Ennio never went to culinary school, he was the most schooled and skilled man I ever met at food and service. He was a master at making guests feel welcome; his presence was contagious. He was tough, fair, and most of all, fun—even while we were working endless days.

Chef Riga was a leader. He had a passion for teaching talented people who wanted to advance themselves. He hired young cooks right out of culinary school and groomed them to be chefs.

Many of Riga's mentees ended up owning their own restaurants, no doubt experiencing even greater levels of success because of his teachings.

I would randomly run into people who worked with Chef Riga, and many owed much of their success to what they had learned from him. Ennio was a humble and brilliant man who brought success to both the people and the restaurants in which he worked. If I could have, I would have worked for Ennio my entire career.

Here are just a few of the things I learned from Ennio:

- Passion is the foundation of cooking; if you don't have it for the restaurant business, you should not be in it.
- Respect everyone, from the dishwasher to the CEO, and make everyone feel important. Look them in the face and show them you are interested in learning who they are. Take care of everyone in a way that shows you are happy to have them on your team.
- Pay attention to details—to execute successfully, you must be prepared.
- Never stop learning, and learn as much as you can while you can.
- Table service and wine pairing is not just a job—it's an art form.
- Do not let others intimidate you.
- Develop others; keep an eye out for talent, and then groom them for success.

- Food cost drives a restaurant's financial success; mind your waste; inspect the garbage to know what is being thrown away.
- Being a restaurateur is all about the guest.
- Be real and honest, and learn how to read people.

William Kuruc's Reflections

I worked with Ennio at Prime Hospitality as a regional chef and learned so much from him: uplifting, passion, friend, presence, personality, determination, thunderstorm, magician, flambé.

He was a true restaurateur who knew the front and back of the house.

We traveled a lot together, opening up many restaurants. He would always come in like a thunderstorm. After all, Ennio was the corporate chef, in charge of food cost, menus, staff, and overall food quality. He meant business and was a force to be reckoned with. He made everyone feel welcome while remaining firmly committed to excellence.

"I am a humble man—and I am a national treasure!" This is my favorite Ennio-ism.

Many times, we were sent in to check on things that were not going right. Ennio taught me to be calm in the face of adversity. He thought one step ahead of everyone else with incredible foresight. He helped set the stage for people to succeed by coaching them, so that potential issues became non-issues.

Ennio to the rescue was sort of the norm. Many times, he would be called in to help with difficult situations and took us along as a superhero team to save the day, often working around the clock.

One time we had to rescue a dinner for fifteen hundred people. The chef and three other people quit, but in our business, the show must go on, and that was our shared attitude. We would all pile in Ennio's van and go. When we would arrive, it was like a well-oiled machine. Ennio would start organizing, appoint people to positions, and then we'd work like crazy till the job was done.

You can't quite describe the fun you're having with Ennio, because you're delirious after working so many hours, but his great personality saved the day, in more ways than one. I only hope some of that rubbed off on me. If I could work with him again, I'd do it in a heartbeat. He knew how to be a harda**, yet he treated us, me and Bob, really well, so we respected him tremendously.

CHAPTER 7

— ❦ —

Retirement to Florida and My Fight Against Cancer, 2004–2016

AT SIXTY-FIVE, I realized it was time to slow down. I had worked for so many years. Doors at Prime Hospitality started closing. I worked part-time until I retired. A wonderful time in my life ended and something new began. My excellent staff threw an amazing retirement party (yes, banquet-style). So many people came to wish me goodbye. It meant so much that they came to celebrate with me.

Shortly thereafter, we sold the house we had raised our children in and moved to Florida. Julie and Debbie were married, and my wife and I wanted to experience a new life. We moved to Lake Worth, Florida, to a brilliant retirement community, Bellaggio, with all the amenities you can imagine. Rose and I were very active. We really enjoyed ourselves; in fact, we were popular in the neighborhood. Why? Well, we did it up *Riga style* once again. We entertained a lot. We would invite the neighbors over for dinner and canasta. We had big banquet-style parties as well. One New Year's Eve, we had an amazing party: more than fifty people. For a while, it was the talk of the community. Entertaining is what I did best, and this was something our neighbors really looked forward to…and we had fun doing it.

We bought new furniture and spent a lot of time making this home our new paradise. We embraced retirement head-on. I did more gardening: herbs, tomatoes…I even started planting trees: avocado, fig, orange, banana.

I got more involved with the Bellaggio community, joining Citizens on Patrol (COP) about two days a week; I really enjoyed this. I also met my dear friend Steve. It was our job to keep the neighborhood safe. We drove in a special car, and I even wore a uniform, which was fun for me.

Steve and I also enjoyed discussing God's ways and many blessings. Steve introduced me to Christ Fellowship Church in Royal Palm Beach. What a great place! I really enjoyed the services, and when I became sick, the pastors came to my house to pray with me.

I helped the community as much as I could…I catered a few local events, joined the Italian Club, and even took a lead role in bringing Flakowitz to Bellaggio. I knew the owner from New Jersey, and we had long discussed bringing this in. I helped with everything from menu creation to portions to pricing. This was fun for me, as I got to use my talents again. Working was such a big part of my life; in retrospect, I probably should have never stopped working completely, as it kept me alive and vibrant.

I took a few trips to Italy during this time as well. It was important to see my nephews and spend time with their children.

I loved my family so much, and it was so hard to live in another country. I missed much of their lives, but I kept in touch as much as I could. Fabrizio was like a son to me, and I wanted him to know how proud I was of him.

I also spent more time fishing. It was so peaceful to be out on the water and in touch with nature. Two good friends, Aaron Greenburg and Rick Gross, loved to fish with me. Both had boats, and I would fish with them when time allowed. I never went without a ton of sandwiches: mortadella, salami, provolone, and other Italian specialties…always a feast. So many good times on the boat fishing for striped bass, fluke, and whatever else came our way.

Fishing also brought me food to cook. I remember when Sharon and Rick came to visit me from a Key West trip. They brought me so many fish! Even though I was not feeling well, I whipped up some fish for everyone. As time went on, though, I felt weaker and weaker and cooked less and less. Sharon and Rick were dear friends of ours, and we had raised our children together. So many memories.

During my restaurant days, I had met the Deleasa family. Bucky, Danielle, Michael, and Dina were such special children, and I was the best chef in the world for them.

Angela, Danielle's mother, is a very nice lady. She is also a good cook. When I had the restaurant, one of my greatest experiences was taking care of them. They used to come to the restaurant every few weeks, and sometimes they would have parties there.

When Danielle got engaged, it meant so much for Rose and me to be invited to her wedding. (Kevin and Danielle later starred in their own E! reality series, *Married to Jonas*, which aired in 2012.) The wedding was held at the Oheka Castle in Huntington, New York, on December 19, 2009. That weekend, however, brought one of the worst winter blizzards. Because of that, we couldn't drive; we had to take the bus. I was supposed to cook for them, but it didn't end up working out, and I was so disappointed. When we arrived, they checked everyone for cameras. I sat with my wife and some stars, like Christian music icon Michael W. Smith. As we were sitting at the table and the beautiful wedding unfolded, the snowstorm was still brewing. We ended up only having an appetizer, because the bus was leaving.

Years before, I bet Bucky that if I lost fifty pounds, he and Angela would give me $1,000. They were always very generous; once they gave me a $600 watch. On their daughter's wedding day, I wanted to give back for their kindness. The bus took six hours to get to the hotel because of the storm, so I wasn't able to cook for such a special couple. It wasn't their fault, but I couldn't do my fruit flambé show, as I had promised Danielle (traveling all the way from Florida to do it). It just didn't work out.

The Deleasas are such a nice family. Kevin Jonas married not just a beautiful girl, but also a very special woman. Kevin, make her happy. A happy family is the most important dream we can achieve in life.

In 2010, it hurt a lot to breathe. I learned that I had developed chronic obstructive pulmonary disease (COPD). Doctors gave me a breathing machine and a lot of medication. I really started to slow down then. Rose and I started going to the arcades more, winning so many gift cards for our kids, as well as for groceries (given our fixed income). The arcade, I could do. They pump air into these places, and somehow, it makes you feel good. I also loved the rush of winning.

Around 2012, I started to get very sick with fevers. Shortly after, I was diagnosed with stage 4 lung cancer. I went through chemo and radiation and biopsies…got positron emission tomography (PET) scans and computed tomography (CT) scans every three to four months…and let me tell you, this was tough.

I went for radiation every day for four months. No matter how sick I got, I never stopped encouraging the other sick people

I encountered. I would talk with them and share how God was fighting with us to beat this.

In October 2014, my wife got sick with a blood infection, and I was very sick at home. My daughter Julie came to help us. I have never seen anyone move so fast. She went from the hospital to come home to care for me. She told me that this was the hardest week of her life. Luckily, my wife got better, and I qualified for long-term healthcare benefits. We were able to get a nurse to come and assist me at the house five days a week, from nine to five. I would like to thank several great nurses who cared for me so kindly, especially Maria, who was with me the longest. Thank you for helping me document my life story. It was so, so kind of you to do this. I was able to send my daughter the email with my typed stories reflected here.

Time was running short, but I was still fighting and staying very close to God. All my friends came to visit during this time; somehow, I still managed to cook for everyone. Friends, family, and former coworkers came to visit and even stay.

My life has been comprised of amazing people and marvelous experiences. I grew up as a young poor boy during World War II in Italy and encountered so many different lives. I have loved and worked hard.

I want to pass along my passion for the job, people, family, and friends, plus my love for Jesus and all the saints in paradise.

So please: whatever you do in life, do it with passion. Consider it as your gift to God, in return for all He has given you. According to the Bible (Mark 12:17), Jesus said, "Give back to Caesar what is Caesar's and to God what is God's."

When you are afraid of something—for example, death—realize that you can stay on course and push forward. Why am I not afraid of anything? I am a little man from a little village in Italy. It takes courage. It is just a mental block when people say, "I cannot do it." Yes, you *can* do it! We are responsible for our own lives. My father told me, when I was young, that I had to go to work...so I went to work. When you have no choice, it's like being thrown into an ocean; you must learn to swim, and fast. I have terminal cancer. I have gone through so much on this course of my life. But I have always stayed on course...and I refuse to die before I finish this book.

Whatever you do in life, do it with passion and care. If you are a waiter, do it with care. When you're cooking tableside, look at your customers and learn what they like. If you are making a spicy dish, ask your customers if they like spicy food. If not, make it less spicy. You want them to enjoy what you are making for them. Cooking tableside is an art, but *whatever you do in life, try the best you can, and become an expert at something.* As long as you try with passion and selflessness, you can achieve your goals. This is true of anything—not just cooking.

Be prepared, because everybody will die someday. I would love to cook for God and all the saints in paradise. People used to tell me that my food was made for the gods. I want to cook for Jesus, Maria Esperanza, Padre Pio, Joseph, and Mary.

My message is simple: *have passion, faith, love, and fun.* Set a course for your life as I did. My course was first to provide for my family, to make people feel welcome and happy with food, and finally to leave a legacy. My children and grandchildren and all the people I encountered and helped are my legacy.

I hope you have enjoyed learning of my journey, and *I wish you blessings, favor, and hope* on your own journey. Enjoy the small moments and relish the big ones. Our life is a series of moments that will one day translate into eternity.

God bless you.

❧

Julie's Reflections

Mom and Dad came home from a Florida trip and told me that they had bought a house and were moving there. I was thirty-three, and as happy as I was for them, I was not ready for them to leave me. Is any child really ready for that? It complicated things.

After my parents retired to Florida, I would visit as often and as much I could. That was a magical time. I have such vivid memories of my dad waiting to pick me up from the airport—and how he greeted me like I was the most important person in the world.

From the first day we arrived, we had the same meal over and over: seafood salad and tuna for lunch, and his amazing ribs for dinner. We almost always had some sort of lobster or crab also. Dad went all out for breakfast: bacon, eggs, and bagels. He wanted to spoil us, because I think he missed cooking for me. I was also going through a very tough time in my life, so time with my dad was a retreat from all that.

Steve Pristas's Reflections

In 2003, a year after my wife Judie and I moved to the Bellaggio active-adult community in Lake Worth, Florida, I met Ennio Riga. We both joined the Bellaggio's Citizens Observer Patrol (COPS) and Community Emer-gency Response Team (CERT) team. CERT prepared and trained us to handle hurricane or tornado aftermaths.

When Ennio went on patrol by himself, things seemed to happen. For instance, while patrolling the local shopping center, Ennio saw a car parked in a fire lane, windows closed, engine not running, ninety degrees out, with a small child in the back seat. Ennio parked the COP car, went into the liquor store, pulled the mother out, and gave her a talking-to. Another time, in the same shopping center, he drove directly into a bank robbery in process. Our COP unit received a "Unit of the Year" award while Ennio was still a member.

The last year of his life, I took Ennio to church on Wednesday evenings for prayer service. While Ennio was confined to home, a pastor agreed to visit, to talk about what was going to happen. Ennio was reclining in his easy chair with his eyes closed. When he opened his eyes, Jesus was standing before him! (Actually, the pastor looked like Jesus). Ennio, overjoyed, said he couldn't wait to get to heaven to cook for Him.

Rose Riga's Reflections

Once in a lifetime, if you're lucky, you get a chance to be loved by someone great. Someone who adores you, and someone who is committed to you till death do you part, in sickness and in health, and through the joy and struggles of life. Ennio and I had a beautiful marriage. From the moment I met Ennio, I was taken by his energy. He stood with me through all the hard times and all the good times. The truth is, life gets ugly, but it is always a little sweeter with someone to share it with. That was Ennio. We fought a lot and loved each other more. We traveled to Italy together, and all over the country, and spent many weekends in Atlantic City.

Ennio
&
Rose

We retired to Florida about fourteen years ago, and since then our relationship grew stronger. We really did almost everything together. We went food shopping, cooked, and entertained friends and family. We went to the arcade, casino, and the movies; we shopped and went out to dinner. We enjoyed our retirement. He deserved this time, as he really worked so hard.

I sure did get good at being a sous chef. I cut, peeled, and prepped food, and then I had the luxury of cleaning all the pots. He used every pot and every mixing spoon just about every time he cooked. Retirement was just a long party until Ennio became sick. We entertained in our amazing Florida villa. Ennio called it paradise, and he was so engaged in our new life.

The last year was very hard for all of us. Ennio was tired. He coughed a lot; he fought the good fight. It was very hard to see him like this; it was hard to accept that the life I knew with my husband was going to end. He fought and prayed and went to church…and I noticed that he was even more spiritual at the end. He made his peace with this life and the people he loved, and somehow, he was ready for his next journey: heaven. Hospice came and was with him around the clock. We tried so hard to keep him; we really did.

On February 12, Ennio passed away at home with the assistance of hospice and my daughter Debbie. Julie stayed close by on the phone with him as much as she could from New Jersey. He was surrounded by love, and was visited by family and friends who said their last goodbyes to him. My lifelong love was gone. You don't realize how much of yourself dies when you lose your love. Now I have a lifetime of memories. Not a day that goes by that I do not think of him. I live in the home where we were together, and his presence is all around me and in my heart.

May God bless each and every one of you reading this. May my husband Ennio rest in peace, and may I be reunited with him one day.

Devorah Riga's Reflections

After several years of my father's fight with cancer, it was time to experience the last days with him. Faced with the choice of having him spend the last days at home or in the hospital, my family was leaning toward bringing him to the hospital. One week before, however, when my father was able to utter his last words, he had requested that he be able to die at home.

I immediately spoke up on my father's behalf and said we were staying home and that I would be there every step of the way. My mother was not able to really be there the way I could, and my sister in New Jersey felt that she wanted her last memory of my dad to be one of strength. I respected their ways of grieving about this.

This man was known for his passion for life, and it was traumatic to see him at this stage of existence, close to the end. Julie was still able to Face Time with him for hours, and we all cherished our last time together as a family. My father was the rock of the family and had an unwavering faith and strength, so to see him this way was extremely painful.

My father loved me but never understood what I did. A doula of birth, life, and transfiguration, I assist the soul's entrance into this world, how to navigate through life, and finally, how to cross over into the next part of its journey. I knew I could do this for him.

I laid with him in bed as I had done when I was five years old, and I just emanated the love a daughter has for her father; he did the same. Hospice made him as comfortable as they could; however, a few days later, he stopped speaking and was sleeping most of the day. He had a few visitors, mostly his good friends.

I connected with my father during that time in a way that I had never done before. It was as if our souls finally met and understood. Every past fight and incident where we did not meet eye to eye just fell away, and all that was left was love. We were just two souls connecting now. As each of his senses began to fade, I concentrated on just breathing with him.

I stayed with him day and night, telling him stories of the world to come, how we were always a team, how our connection would only get stronger, and what it meant to let go of the body. His eyes opened wide as he listened to these tales with excitement. I played music with resonating frequencies to aid in the expansion and release process. We transcended any differences we had, and at the end, it was just love. He taught me that the only thing we take to the next world is our connection; everything else stays behind.

The last day was mostly about breath. When his breathing changed, the hospice nurse let me know that his time was approaching, and so I just held him and breathed. His breathing normalized and slowed, and Spirit let me know these were the last ones we would breathe together. I took one last breath with the man who walked me through this world, and now I was walking with him as he passed over. As we both exhaled, he ascended.

When my father let go of his body, I felt his soul go through mine and saw him on the other side. He was vibrant and young, and many were waiting for him. Bathed in a golden light, my father passed over. I stayed with his body for a while before telling anyone he was gone. The first person I called was my sister. I told her Dad is everywhere, and she said, "How can he be everywhere?" Just then, the light in the room flashed, and the CD player that had been playing soft music for five days straight suddenly stopped. Apparently, the lights in my sister's house in New Jersey flashed too, and a picture of my father appeared, smiling, on her computer screen.

I then replied, "That's how he can be everywhere."

My father is still with me, and our connection has only grown. He has sent me messages through others. At his memorial service, it was mentioned that once he said he was going to cook pasta for everyone in heaven. A week later, a woman who only met me once before told me she smelled pasta sauce when a chef showed up to give me a message that my father was breathing fine, and not in any pain, and was cooking for heaven.

My sister was skeptical about these messages, because she did not receive any. I told her, "Julie, give him an opening and he will come."

She finally did, and said, "Dad if you are here, play 'Volare' on the radio"…and seconds later, my sister heard the sounds of my father's favorite song.

Ennio Giuseppe Riga, we will all love you forever.

Jamison (Jamie) Waugh's Reflections

I did not get a chance to know Ennio as well as I would have liked, because his time was short after we met. I thought he was kind and genuine. He was happy to meet me, and was even happier at the thought of me marrying his daughter. He wanted to make sure she was taken care of and was thankful that I came into Julie's life. I was privileged to eat his food when we visited Florida. His marinara sauce with crab was absolutely amazing!

ԳԲ

Fabrizio Morasutto's Reflections

(Fabrizio is my father's nephew in Italy and was like a son to my father.)

My Zio could not wait to come to Italy to spend time around the fields to be in touch with nature and animals and, of course, meet his friends. Together we visited the places of our childhood, but most of all when Ennio visited, he loved to just spend time with his parents.

My Uncle used to visit Zompicchia during the time of the country fair and was invited to many friends' parties. We spent long days fishing the little rivers near home.

Zio loved cooking for us and helping my mother care for the vegetable garden. Most importantly, Ennio was my guide and mentor. He not only offered suggestions on my career and personal life, but also helped me believe in everything I did and his love and guidance gave me the courage to believe in myself. We just enjoyed doing simple things of life and just chatting for hours. I owe many of my successes to Uncle Ennio and I think about him every day.

Joyce Boll's Reflections

Ennio was love at first sight for me and my family. His deep loving eyes, that smile, and his Italian accent was enough to stop you in your tracks and listen to anything he said. Add food to the equation, and everyone welcomed him into our loud Jewish family (and yes, he did fit in).

When I met him, he was wearing a navy blue and white horizontal striped long-sleeved shirt with white pants, like Gene Kelly in *An American in Paris*. I had a cold, so my mom wouldn't let me run around outside. I watched him from the den window while he did delightful futbol tricks in our yard.

Ennio was known for his amazing Livingston parties with *la famiglia*. We ate sumptuous dishes and watched Ennio dance and sing while expertly cutting up pineapples and bananas. I was thrilled that he had a chance to meet my daughter before he passed. Watching him sing and laugh with her was one of my most treasured moments.

Ennio told me I was powerful and courageous. ("You got the biggest balls in this family!" he said to me.) He said I was not like the rest. He inspired me to reach for the stars because he knew I would always succeed.

And such an amazing chef and fisherman! He prepared fresh fish he caught that day with tomatoes and anise salad, fried zucchini flowers, pasta e fagiole soup, and let's never forget the osso buco!

He brought all walks of life to his table. He celebrated life and lived in the moment…and it inspired me to live my own life with passion and courage.

Alyse Merritt's Reflections

I remember being at Julie's house countless times where I was discouraged as a teen, especially due to hardships with my own family, even challenging relationships with "silly boys" at school… and Ennio was always there for me—guiding me, advising me, loving me, reassuring me. It meant the world to me.

As Julie and I would write spiritual songs together, and Julie would belt them out beautifully and soulfully for all to hear, Ennio was her loudest cheerleader, her biggest fan, and the first to cast out any sense of rejection.

Ennio was a supreme believer in Julie and Debbie's greatness and talent, a dispeller of negativity and criticism, and a visionary who saw the unique and beautiful potential in all of us.

Ennio made us all strive higher, yearn deeper, and believe there are no bounds to being the best we could possibly be.

For me personally, Ennio was also an open heart and a listening ear. Never judgment or condemnation. No preconceived notions...only love.

Such candor and wisdom, providing kindness, compassion, and, of course, the most delicious, amazing comfort foods. From his five-star breaded mac and cheese, to fettuccine Alfredo, to quickly whipping up mashed potatoes when I was down...he just always knew the right words to say and the perfect foods to share.

As I grew older, Ennio still played a pivotal role. One day in Ennio's kitchen, while I was hanging out with Julie, I let everyone know, quite shockingly, that I had been proposed to by two different men that week, both of whom I thought I loved deeply. I asked Ennio, "I am so confused; which one should I marry?"

Ennio just looked at me with those steely blue eyes and said, "Neither! They are both terrible for you! A better one is in your future!"

As always, he turned out to be right.

One year later, when my mother was stricken with cancer and about to die, Ennio told me how he envisioned my mother entering the gates of heaven. He continually provided my father and me with such peace and comfort. All the while, Ennio also sustained us with warm, freshly prepared meals.

When my beloved father was dying in Ennio and Rose's same town, Ennio called to reassure me that they would be with me to the very end.

After, Ennio offered me and my brother a place to stay. He cooked for us, offered to prepare food for my father's funeral, and provided constant support and unconditional love. I am forever indebted to Ennio Riga, a world-class chef and man.

Claudia Coscarello's Reflections

I didn't know Ennio as long as the family knows Ennio, but I was privileged to call him a friend…He was compassionate and always very funny. Whenever we would gather at the table, Ennio always had a silly story to tell us. He was the focus of the light around the table: funny, very giddy, very positive…never malicious or negative. He knew how to make people feel welcome and special, as well as how to include people.

He also told me it felt so good to come here, because he knew he could get a good meal and he didn't have to cook it himself!

Aaron Greenberg's Reflections

I met Ennio in 1977. Our wives worked together at a hair salon called Flo's in Hillside, New Jersey, and we all became friends. He was fun to be around and was truly genuine. We became such good friends of the Riga's that we were like family.

I have so many memories, over the years, of all of the places where Ennio worked, even of visiting him in Italy. We spent many Saturday nights at Riga's Restaurant in East Orange. We loved to visit him there, and he treated us like kings. Ennio would always make me my favorite meal: veal Parmesan on the bone, and mussels as the appetizer. He always made us feel like we were at home.

Ennio and I spent many a day fishing together and just laughing about life. He would always bring Italian sandwiches to eat on the boat. Every time he would catch a fish, he would say, "That's a keeper." Throughout all the trials and joys of life, we were always there for each other. Ennio was the most unforgettable character I ever met—and a once-in-a-lifetime friend.

Epilogue

Stay on Course
The Life and Legacy of Ennio Riga, "Chef to the Stars"

LEAD, LOVE, LIVE

IT WAS MY pleasure to provide you with my father's life story. As I reflect on all of the time and love that went into this book, my one wish is that you are changed for good reading it, and that you got to know Chef Ennio Riga.

Dad always had a secret ingredient to his recipes. This secret ingredient was what set his food apart from all of the others. As you have read in his stories and lessons, he also had many secret ingredients to a rich, full life.

To conclude this book, let me bring up legacy again. This is where you will find the thread of my dad's life continuing…because of all he imparted to others along the way.

I asked several people I've mentored along the way if knowing me has helped them on their journey. I did this to see if my dad's influence on me continued and still held true. I asked, "What did you learn from me?" The answers were exciting. They told me all about passion, fun, service, and doing good for others. Suddenly, it all came together. These were all the things my dad had taught me. Wow!

In that moment, I got it. I finally understood what Dad was really saying when he said *Stay on Course,* and here is the takeaway.

When Dad said, "My daughter, stay on course," he was really saying:

- Have courage. Life is going to knock you down time and time again. Get up, brush it off, and keep going.
- Have faith—all of this is for a bigger purpose. You are here for a mission, so find out what your purpose is, and pray!

- Be real with people; let them see you.
- Develop your talents. Excel at what you do!
- Develop a passion for service. If your heart is in the right place, everything becomes easier. Always consider how you are adding value to others.
- Have fun on your journey, and be present.
- Be a leader! Leadership is about service to others. What sustains the heart of a leader is developing and nurturing the next generation of leaders. My dad's life extends and lives on timelessly through the generations that follow.

Dad, thank you for all that you imparted to future generations and to me. When you said I was in charge of your legacy, only now am I beginning to understand what that means. What you were saying was, I need to stay on course so that I can be there for our family, just as *you* were there for our family. I also realize it's now *my* turn to lead, mentor, and coach the next generation and encourage them for good. I will devote my full heart to this effort, and always remember…that if the world falls down on my shoulders, I will brush it off and keep going. I will stay on course, just as you have stayed on course, and so continue your legacy. I thank you for this gift you have left me, and I will carry you with me in my heart wherever I go and bring your encouragement to others through all that I do. I love you, Dad, and I look forward to the day we meet again!

This Is Not Goodbye—Just a Breath Before the Next Hello

A legacy to be remembered!
Stay on Course and never give up!

- Love with your whole heart, and be passionate.
- Lead your life as an act of service to others, so that they in turn may lead others, creating a legacy to be remembered.
- Live without taking yourself too seriously; have fun, glorify in your silliness, and laugh out loud.

Come...we go right *now!*
Andiamo

Ennio's Wall of Fame Stars

1. Allen, Peter *(1944–1992)*
2. Alpert, Herb *(1935–)*
3. Anka, Paul *(1941–)*
4. Bassey, Shirley *(1937–)*
5. Bennett, Tony *(1926–)*
6. Benvenuti, Nino *(1938–)*
7. Bishop, Joey *(1918–2007)*
8. Burton, Richard *(1925–1984)*
9. Bush, George H. W. *(1924–)*
10. Carney, Art *(1918–2003)*
11. Caron, Jacques *(1940–)*
12. Carson, Johnny *(1925–2005)*
13. Carter, Jack *(1922–2015)*
14. Cassavetes, John *(1929–1989)*
15. Cavett, Dick *(1936–)*
16. Chaplin, Charlie *(1889–1977)*
17. Dangerfield, Rodney *(1921–2004)*
18. Deleasa, Bucky
19. DeLuise, Dom *(1933–2009)*
20. Douglas, Mike *(1920–2006)*
21. Easton, Sheena *(1959–)*
22. Elizabeth, Queen *(1926–)*
23. Ely, Ronald *(1938-)*
24. Esperanza, Maria *(1928–2004)*
25. Falana, Lola *(1942–)*
26. Fisher, Eddie *(1928–2010)*
27. Fitzgerald, Ella *(1917–1996)*
28. Franklin, Joe *(1926–2015)*
29. Frost, David *(1939–2013)*
30. Garvey, Cindy *(1949-)*
31. Gazzara, Ben *(1930–2012)*

32. Gibb, Andy *(1958–1988)*
33. Griffin, Merv *(1925–2007)*
34. Harris, Franco *(1950–)*
35. Heston, Charlton *(1923–2008)*
36. Hope, Bob *(1903–2003)*
37. Hussein bin Talal, King of Jordan *(1935–1999)*
38. Iglesias, Julio *(1943–)*
39. Jagger, Mick *(1943–)*
40. Jonas, Kevin (and Danielle) *(1987–) (1986–)*
41. Jones, Davy (and the Monkees) *(1945–2012)*
42. Jones, Jack *(1938–)*
43. Jones, Tom *(1940–)*
44. Kean, Tom *(1935–)*
45. Kennedy, Edward (Ted) *(1932–2009)*
46. Kennedy, Jackie *(1929–1994)*
47. Kennedy, Robert *(1925–1968)*
48. King, Alan *(1927–2004)*
49. Lemaire, Jacques (New Jersey Devils) *(1945–)*
50. Lamoriello, Lou (1942-)
51. Liberace, Władziu Valentino *(1919–1987)*
52. Lollobrigida, Gina *(1927–)*
53. Lombardi, Vince *(1913–1970)*
54. Manna, Charlie *(1920–1971)*
55. Mathis, Johnny *(1935–)*
56. Meir, Golda *(1898–1978)*
57. Minnelli, Liza *(1946–)*
58. Nixon, Richard M. *(1913–1994)*
59. Newmar, Julie *(1933–)*
60. Newton, Wayne *(1942–)*
61. Orlando, Tony *(1944–)*
62. Paola of Belgium, Queen *(1937–)*
63. Pavarotti, Luciano *(1935–2007)*
64. Philbin, Regis *(1931–)*
65. Philippe, King of the Belgians *(1960–)*
66. Reiner, Rob (1947-)
67. Reynolds, Debbie *(1932–2016)*
68. Rickles, Don *(1926–2017)*
69. Rivers, Joan *(1933–2014)*

70. Rizzuto, Phil *(1917–2007)*
71. Robinson, Larry (New Jersey Devils) *(1951–)*
72. Rockefeller, Nelson *(1908–1979)*
73. Rowlands, Gena *(1930–)*
74. Sellers, Peter *(1925–1980)*
75. Sinatra, Frank *(1915–1998)*
76. Sinatra, Nancy *(1940–)*
77. Stevens, Connie *(1938–)*
78. Stuarti, Enzo *(1919–2005)*
79. Summer, Donna *(1948–2012)*
80. Taylor, Elizabeth *(1932–2011)*
81. Teresa, Mother *(1910–1997)*
82. Thomas, Danny *(1912–1991)*
83. Tose, Leonard *(1915–2003)*
84. Valli, Frankie *(1934–)*
85. Vinton, Bobby *(1935–)*
86. Warwick, Dionne *(1940–)*
87. Williams, Anson *(1949–)*
88. Wolf, Warner *(1937–)*

Recipe Index

Made in the USA
Columbia, SC
19 April 2021